Lilies & Clover

Lilies & Clover

A novel by

Shelly Johnson-Choong

BOOKCRAFT
Salt Lake City, Utah

All characters in this book are fictitious,
and any resemblance to actual persons,
living or dead, is purely coincidental.

Library of Congress Catalog Card Number 97-77972
ISBN 1-57008-398-3

First Printing, 1998

Printed in the United States of America

For my mother, who taught me to walk in the light.

CHAPTER 1

Jimmy Lee stared in disbelief as Mitch strode off. They had been together ever since her sixteenth birthday over a year ago, and now he was walking away from her.

How could this be? She was willing to admit that lately things had been difficult between them. Mitch wasn't a Mormon and he had no interest in the Church, and for the last couple of months he had campaigned for a more physical relationship. Those things had bitterly disappointed her, but that didn't change her feelings for him. She loved him, and she had always believed that they would work it out. Now that chance was walking away from her.

With unblinking eyes she watched as he left the library and walked into the hall. She still sat in the far corner of the library, where he had asked to meet her. It was one of the few places on campus where they could have a little privacy. When Mitch had asked to meet with her she had thought nothing of it; he probably just wanted to firm up Friday night's date, she supposed, or maybe he was struggling with one of his new classes. She had tutored him in math. But in the library she had sat in stunned silence and listened to his carefully rehearsed speech about needing space and wanting to date other girls.

Jimmy Lee had no rebuttal. She wasn't prepared. So she had leaned against the table and listened with mute shock. Then Mitch had risen from his chair and walked away. The whole monologue probably took three minutes, and yet it had left her devastated.

Jimmy Lee jumped as the tardy bell rang. It was the first day of the winter semester and she wasn't even sure what class she was supposed to be attending. Swallowing hard, she searched her notebook until she found her schedule. She looked over the list of classes. Chemistry III. Great! One of her tougher classes! Sighing, she stood and straightened her books. She was too stunned to cry. It still felt unreal.

With deliberate steps she walked out into the almost empty hallway. A few kids were scurrying to their classes. A couple of them flashed Jimmy Lee a smile but she didn't smile back. Instead she concentrated on getting to her next class. A few minutes ago it had been just another class, but now just walking in the science building was a monumental task. It was the habit that kept her moving.

Finally she made it to the right room. The teacher, Mr. Bradley, gave her a long look as she walked in, but he continued with his lecture. Quietly Jimmy Lee settled into the seat next to another student. Without much thought, she set her books on the table. They tumbled onto the floor with a loud racket.

Mr. Bradley gave her a harder look. "See me after class," he said before continuing with his talk. Her mouth went dry as she nodded. Then she bent over to pick up her books—and cracked skulls with the boy sitting next to her, who had also bent over at the same time to help.

She didn't cry out for fear of angering the teacher even more, but tears came to her eyes. She willed them away, afraid that once the tears got started they would never stop. She was right. Slowly the tears leaked from her. She saw the concern in the student sitting next to her, a red-haired kid with freckles. He kept glancing at her, and when she fumbled around her notebook, looking for a tissue, he deftly handed her a handkerchief. Jimmy Lee took the piece of cloth and wiped her eyes. She wished she could blow her nose but didn't feel right about using his handkerchief for that. She settled for wiping her eyes and tried to concentrate on the lecture.

After class, Jimmy Lee waited for the students to disperse

before walking up to the front of the classroom. Mr. Bradley sat at his desk. Jimmy Lee knew he was waiting for her to make her excuse for her tardiness and disruptive behavior.

Jimmy Lee cleared her throat. "I'm sorry," she said. "I got distracted. It won't happen again."

Mr. Bradley's features softened. "See that it doesn't," he said. "How's your head?"

She rubbed the spot where a lump was beginning to form. It was tender. "It'll be okay," she said.

"Maybe you should see the school nurse and get a bag of ice. I wanted to tell Kody that too, but he left before I got the chance. The two of you really smashed into each other."

"If I see him, I'll mention it," Jimmy said.

Jimmy Lee said good-bye to Mr. Bradley and walked out of the science lab. Her head felt like a cracked egg and it throbbed with every heartbeat. She didn't even see the red-haired kid leaning against the wall.

"You okay?" he asked as he pushed himself away from the wall and fell in step with her.

She nodded. "I'm fine. How about you?"

Kody grinned. "My head is as hard as cement. I'm sure you got the raw end of our collision."

"If your name is Kody, Mr. Bradley suggested that we go to the school nurse and get a bag of ice. Do you need one?"

"My name *is* Kody. Kody McLaughlin, and you're Jimmy Lee Donovan. I don't need a bag of ice. How about you?"

"No," she lied. A bag of ice would feel good. Maybe it would numb the pain in her heart as well.

Kody squinted at her. "Are you sure you're okay? You don't look so good. Maybe you have a concussion or fractured skull. We hit pretty hard."

She noticed that he looked genuinely worried. She shook her head. "No. Only a fractured heart. Thanks for letting me borrow the handkerchief. I'm sorry it got so wet."

"You weren't crying over our accident, were you," Kody said quietly.

Tears surfaced once again. "No." Her voice was shaky. "Mitch and I broke up." Just saying the words made her wince. They sounded so new and foreign.

"Oh, I'm sorry," Kody said softly. "I had no idea." He changed the subject. "What's your next class?"

"Sociology. How about you?"

"Same," Kody said.

They managed to walk into the classroom together, just as the tardy bell rang. In spite of Jimmy Lee's throbbing head she was glad that she wouldn't have to do any explaining to Mr. Sandival. She and Kody managed to find two seats, but they weren't together.

Kody hated to leave Jimmy Lee. She might need his handkerchief again, or maybe his shoulder to cry on. He didn't know Jimmy Lee very well but he did know that her reputation was impeccable.

Jimmy Lee was a strange name for a girl but it somehow fit in this case. Her light brown hair was cut short, and her clear skin had a scrubbed look about it, suggesting that she didn't wear much makeup. Baggy jeans, flannel shirts, and cowboy boots with polished brass tips added to her tomboyish look. She wasn't the prettiest girl in school. In fact, she was plain. Still, everywhere Jimmy Lee went she seemed to spread fresh air and sunshine. People were drawn to her. Kody wasn't the only one to think so. Mitch had always been by her side, and whenever Kody had seen them together it looked as if he adored her.

Kody didn't know Mitch, except by sight and reputation. The tall, muscular senior's ability to play basketball wasn't the only reason why Kody admired him, but it was the most important. All his life Kody had longed to play team games. Instead he was a red-headed runt who played the oboe in the band. His unruly red hair and freckled complexion might be conspicuous, but his frame was a non-draw.

After class was over, Kody found Jimmy Lee. She looked worn out. "Feeling any better?" he asked.

"I think I'll go home," Jimmy Lee said quietly. "My head is really starting to pound." She rubbed her forehead. Her skull did hurt, but she didn't know whether it was from the accident or the pent-up tears.

"Can I get you anything?" Kody asked, feeling helpless.

"No. Thanks for everything. I appreciate your help. Will I see you tomorrow?"

Kody grinned. "Absolutely."

With a final wave he hurried to his next class, but it didn't seem right to leave her. He hesitated for a moment and turned to search the milling crowd, but she had disappeared.

Hurrying to her locker, Jimmy Lee scribbled a note for her locker partner and best friend, Reanna Lewis. She stuck it to the inside of the door with a piece of gum she had chewed for that very purpose. Reanna always took her home after school, and Jimmy Lee wanted to make sure her friend would know she had already left. She didn't go into any details. The way the rumor mill worked at Pinecrest, it was very possible that by the time school was over Reanna would know more about the breakup than Jimmy Lee.

With slow, deliberate steps, Jimmy Lee went to the office to call her mother.

When she climbed into the car a few minutes later, Jimmy Lee allowed her body to sink into the seat.

Beth Donovan immediately put her hand on her daughter's forehead. "Are you ill? You sounded terrible on the phone. You don't have a fever." She placed the back of her hand on Jimmy Lee's cheek. "What's happened?"

Once again the unwanted tears began to surface. Jimmy Lee allowed them to run down her cheeks. She couldn't hold them back any longer. "Mitch . . ." She tried to frame her words but the grief was overwhelming. "Mitch wants to date other girls," she finally stammered out before the sobs took over.

Beth reached across the emergency brake and pulled her daughter close. "Oh, honey! I'm so sorry. You must feel awful."

Jimmy Lee nodded against her mother's shoulder as the sobs racked her body.

They sat there for a long minute until Jimmy Lee's cries finally subsided. She pulled away from her mother and slumped against the seat.

Beth put the car in gear and pulled out into the traffic. "Why don't you tell me exactly what happened."

With a halting voice, Jimmy Lee told her mother everything.

Beth covered her daughter's hands with one of her own and Jimmy Lee squeezed her mother's fingers.

"Tomorrow is going to be hard," Jimmy Lee said quietly.

"Yes. But it'll be the worst day. Each day will get a little easier."

Jimmy Lee looked out at the rain-soaked landscape. Nothing would ever be easy again.

CHAPTER 2

The following day, Kody waited anxiously for Jimmy Lee. He was sitting in the chemistry class, where they had met the previous day. Would she come to class? He had considered calling her last night, just to see if she was okay, but he'd thought better of it. He didn't want to appear as if he was trying to move in on her now that Mitch was out of the way.

When she walked into the room Kody let out a long, deep sigh. Suddenly he realized that he had been holding his breath, afraid that Jimmy Lee wouldn't come to class. She gave Kody a fleeting smile as she sat next to him.

Kody was proud. Jimmy Lee could have sat next to anyone in class. The whole school was aware of her and Mitch's breakup, and anyone in the chemistry class would've gladly given her sympathy.

The final bell rang. "How are you feeling?" Kody asked.

"Okay," Jimmy Lee said in a hoarse whisper.

Kody turned his attention to Mr. Bradley, who was announcing that each student would need to find a lab partner. Kody despaired. Well, that was the end of his relationship with Jimmy Lee. He'd never get the opportunity to know her better. She would have any number of students clamoring to be her partner. He kept his eyes on his books, waiting to hear the chair next to him scoot.

"Should we be partners?" Jimmy Lee asked.

Kody looked up. She was looking at *him.* "You mean you and me?" he asked.

"Sure. That is, unless there's someone else you'd rather hook up with. I'll understand if you've already chosen your partner."

"No, no," he stammered. "I think we'd make a great team." Jimmy Lee smiled again.

Mr. Bradley wrote three essay questions on the board and gave the class their reading assignment. The time went fast, and when the bell rang it startled both of them. Kody considered asking about Mitch, but decided that maybe the less said the better. "Why are you taking such brainy classes?" he asked instead.

"I could ask the same of you," Jimmy Lee said.

"My folks want me to get into a really good college so I'm taking a pretty heavy academic load."

"Same here. I'm hoping to get into BYU after graduation."

"BYU. Isn't that a Mormon university?"

Jimmy Lee nodded. "Yeah. It's a pretty good school, too, and it can be kind of hard to get into."

"So, are you a Mormon?"

"Yeah. I am, but Mitch isn't," she said with sad distraction.

Kody followed her gaze. She was scanning the crowded hall, looking for Mitch without even realizing it.

Suddenly she stiffened. Mitch was swaggering down the side hall past the cafeteria with Brenda Timmins draped all over him; a gum-chewing blonde with lots of makeup and her hair sprayed stiff.

Kody instinctively touched Jimmy Lee's elbow and they kept walking. "She's not very pretty," Kody said.

"I don't think it matters," Jimmy Lee replied bitterly.

Kody tried to think of something to say. Everyone was stealing secret looks at Jimmy Lee to see how she was taking it. She lifted her chin proudly and said nothing. As they stepped outside toward the Humanities building a dark-haired girl walked past, pausing long enough to say, "He's a jerk, Jimmy Lee. Forget him."

The sympathy was too much. Tears came to Jimmy Lee's

eyes. "I just wish people would leave me alone," she muttered softly.

Kody felt strangled by his muteness. What could he possibly say that would help Jimmy Lee? "Listen, everyone will get over it," he said awkwardly. "She just wanted to help."

"I know," she sniffed. "But it doesn't help. It just makes it worse. It's better to feel mad. At least then I don't want to cry all the time."

"Just give it a couple of days. Pretty soon everyone will be talking about something else."

Jimmy Lee closed her eyes. "Maybe I could just stay home for a couple of days."

"That would be the worst possible thing to do."

"Why do you say that?"

"Because your absence will just cause more talk and Brenda Timmins will think she's won."

Kody saw a new spark come into Jimmy Lee's eyes, and he continued. "Besides, that would be letting Mitch off the hook. It'll be much easier for him around here if he doesn't have to deal with you for a couple of days. Can't you tell they're just putting on a show?"

Jimmy Lee tightened her jaw. "Well, I certainly don't want to do Brenda Timmins any favors. Or Mitch either, for that matter." She sighed. "I suppose you're right."

The late bell rang.

"Besides, you can't go home now," Kody grinned. "I'm not walking into sociology tardy by myself."

Jimmy Lee nodded. "You're right about that, too. You wouldn't be late if you hadn't been baby-sitting me. I at least owe it to you to go to class so that you don't have to get in trouble by yourself."

They hurried. Mr. Sandival was calling the roll. "Next time I dock five points off your grade," he said.

They nodded contritely and slid into empty seats near the bookcase. Jimmy Lee looked better by the time class was over.

"Are you going to your next class?" Kody asked as he stood up.

"Yeah. I don't want to be a wimp. Besides, I didn't go yesterday, and I don't want to drop the class."

"Good. Then I'll see you tomorrow?"

Jimmy Lee nodded reluctantly.

As Kody backed away he bumped into another boy who was coming down the aisle. Red shame engulfed Kody as he bent down to pick up his books. "Sorry," he mumbled.

"Hey, why don't you watch where you're going?" the angry voice demanded.

Kody looked up. It was Ken Mackley, also from the basketball team.

"Hey, why don't *you!*" Jimmy Lee snapped back as she leaned over to pick up Kody's ruler.

Ken stood up and slung his books on his hip. "Since when have you begun an adoption program for runts, Jimmy Lee?"

"Grow up, Ken, and quit being an insensitive clod," she responded.

"Anything you say, Miss Mormon," Ken replied with a nasty grin, and he turned away.

Jimmy Lee shook her head. "What a jerk! I think he had something to do with Mitch's decision to break up."

Kody wanted to ask Jimmy Lee what she meant, but he didn't trust his voice to come out without squeaking. He felt that his face was scarlet. Jimmy Lee didn't appear the least bit ruffled—only angry. Taking a deep breath he calmed himself. "Well, I'll see you tomorrow," he said.

Sitting in calculus, Kody tried to concentrate on the equations the teacher was writing on the board, but he kept thinking of Jimmy Lee and how quickly she'd defended him. He wished it hadn't been necessary. He felt his face grow hot once again. Ken had called him a runt, and Kody couldn't deny that the label fit.

The dismissal bell rang. Kody was glad this was only the second day of class. He would have to start paying attention if he wanted a good grade. He hurried to his locker and pulled open the door. It was covered in a poster of Jerry Rice, the greatest receiver to play the game. For a moment the noise of the crowded hallway dropped away as Kody studied the poster. The previous Sunday, on television, he had watched Jerry Rice catch a brilliant pass from Steve Young. It had been exhilarating. For those few seconds when the ball hung in the air Kody had been breathless, and then, as if on cue, Jerry Rice had beaten the defender and plucked the ball out of the air. Kody sighed. Wouldn't it be wonderful to have that kind of strength and talent!

Kody heard the locker next to him open.

"Dreamin' again, McLaughlin?" the upper-classman asked.

Kody didn't answer. He pulled out his oboe and home-work. At least the high school football season was over. No more marching in the cold, wet grass until next year. Maybe he would quit band. Then he would never have to march again. The possibility brightened Kody's mood as he boarded the bus.

CHAPTER 3

After school, Jimmy Lee dragged herself toward her locker, hoping her best friend would be there. She needn't have worried. Reanna Lewis met her in the hallway. "How are you feeling today?" Reanna asked anxiously.

Jimmy Lee shrugged. "About the same." Her voice sounded defeated.

Reanna hugged her. "C'mon, I'll take you home. We can talk on the way."

Jimmy Lee nodded. A few minutes later she was sitting in the passenger seat of Reanna's Datsun, watching the small town of Madrone, Oregon, move by. Tears filled her eyes, blurring her vision. "This has been a tough day," she sniffed.

Reanna patted her friend's hand. "I know, but it'll get better. Do you want to talk about it?"

Pulling her coat tight, Jimmy Lee shook her head. "There's nothing really new to say. I saw Mitch with Brenda Timmins this afternoon. They looked real cozy. I hung out with Kody McLaughlin for a couple of classes. If it weren't for him, I probably would have gone home early, but he talked me into staying. Do you know him?"

Reanna thought for a moment. "I'm not sure."

"I think he's in the band. He has red hair and blue eyes. I bet you'd know him if you saw him."

"Oh, maybe I do. He was in my English class last semester, but I never really talked to him. Is he nice?"

"Seems to be. We're partners in chemistry and we have

sociology together too. I really appreciate the way he behaved when I told him about Mitch. He said he was sorry and everything, and then he just dropped it."

"Everybody else will do the same thing after a few days, Jimmy Lee," Reanna said reassuringly. "The two of you have been an item for over a year, and lots of people feel bad about the breakup. Especially considering who he's seeing now. Brenda Timmins! He didn't wait very long did he? I can't believe it."

"I can," Jimmy Lee muttered.

Reanna glanced at her. "Yeah. I guess you're right. I probably shouldn't be so surprised after some of the things you've told me about the last couple of months. I didn't know Mitch could be such a jerk. I shouldn't have set you up with him in the first place."

"Don't blame yourself, Reenie. Deep down inside, Mitch isn't a jerk. We've been together a long time and most of it's been wonderful." Her eyes puddled again. "I'm going to miss him."

"You look tired," Reanna said.

"I'm exhausted. And to think of what I'm going to have to face tomorrow and the next day at school just makes me want to sink."

"It'll be okay," Reanna said. "I'm here for you. Listen, why don't you spend this Friday night with me? We can eat popcorn and watch a couple of videos."

"Let's watch something funny. I don't want any mushy love stories."

"It's a deal," Reanna agreed.

Jimmy Lee smiled wanly at her friend. "Thanks, Reanna. I'll ask my folks, but I'm sure it'll be okay."

As Reanna eased the car into the Donovan driveway, Jimmy Lee could feel the throb in her head and the dullness in her mind. But the strongest sensation was the pain in the middle of her chest. It seemed to radiate from the very center of her body. With each pulse she felt as if her heart was bound by strong cords that kept the pain in its chambers.

Reanna turned off the engine. "Well, here we are," she said quietly. "Do you want me to come in?"

Jimmy Lee shook her head. "No, thanks anyway, Reenie." She leaned over and hugged her. "Thanks for listening to me." When she pulled away from Reanna she saw tears forming in her best friend's eyes. "Oh, now, don't you start! I'll never dry up if you do."

Reanna laughed in spite of the tears. "I'm sorry, Jimmy Lee. I'm sorry about the whole mess. I hate to see you hurting like this."

"I know you do, and I appreciate it."

Jimmy Lee got out of the car and collected her books. "I'll see you in the morning?"

"First thing," Reanna smiled.

Jimmy Lee waved Reanna out of the driveway from her front porch. It was nice that her best friend always took her to school and home again. It beat riding the bus. But now that she was home she didn't want to go into the house. Instead she sank down on the front steps, ignoring the still, January cold. It was already getting dark, shadows were pooling under the large evergreens. She thought about Mitch but kept the tears at bay. Crying wouldn't help her think clearly, and she knew she needed to work through this trauma with a sharp mind.

It had been a wonderful year with Mitch—glamorous and thrilling. Her parents had been openly concerned when it became apparent that the relationship was more than just a casual evening out. She and her mother had several discussions about seriously dating a non-member. Beth Donovan was sure the issue of sex would come up eventually, and Jimmy Lee had just as firmly believed that Mitch would never question her moral standards.

But she'd been wrong. During the last couple of months her relationship with Mitch had definitely taken a turn for the worse. Jimmy Lee had tried to keep the truth away from her folks but suspected they knew. Her defensiveness a couple of times, when Beth had brought it up, was a dead giveaway, wasn't it? Besides that, she admitted, she didn't want to tell her mother because she didn't want to admit it to herself.

Mitch had been sweet—cajoling and patient, saying he wanted to give her time to get used to the idea. It didn't seem like a bad idea, especially with his warm arm around her and his lips moving slowly over her cheek and neck. But a tug of war began inside of her. It became harder to say no, and her reasons for drawing lines became fuzzier. The truth of the matter was, she loved Mitch. Part of her wanted to erase the lines.

She had never talked to her parents about any of her feelings. She didn't even tell Reanna. It was too confusing and embarrassing to explain the pull she felt toward her boyfriend. Instead, she tried to pretend everything was fine. It was a hard act. Her folks were concerned. They wanted to know all kinds of things. What do you talk about? Did you see any other friends? Did you spend any time at Mitch's home? How was the physical side of their relationship? Did he want more? Did she? Jimmy Lee would answer casually, hoping her parents would feel there was no need to worry. But she knew they did, and that added to her own stress and guilt.

When had things become so hard? She and Mitch used to have a great time. Even the autumn was fun—hikes through autumn leaves and evergreen forests, cheering at football games, waiting for the first snowfall in the mountains so they could plan their cross-country ski trips . . .

Wiping her eyes, Jimmy Lee wished she knew which memories would be easier—those good, fun, and loving times or the last couple of months, which had been filled with tension, arguments, and an intangible pressure. She sighed, straightened her books in the crook of her arm, and walked into the house.

Beth Donovan was in the kitchen frosting an apple spice cake. "Hi, honey," she said. "I thought I heard Reanna's car."

Jimmy Lee dumped her books onto the dining room table and sat down at the kitchen bar, the last of her energy dissipating.

Beth put the spatula down. "How was your day?"

Fatigue washed over Jimmy Lee. Even crying was too much of an effort. "It was horrible, Mom. Everyone at school kept looking at me as if they expected me to shatter into a hundred pieces."

"Did anyone say anything to you?"

"Just a couple of people. And everybody's really nice. But I think the news is still getting around. Mitch and Brenda are . . . are . . ."

Beth moved beside her daughter. She nodded understandingly. "They're making a statement." She rubbed Jimmy Lee's arm.

"Something like that."

"Let's think this through. What do you think will happen tomorrow?"

Jimmy Lee shrugged. "I don't know. Either everyone will be laughing at me, or they'll feel sorry for me. I don't like either one of those options. I wish I could skip school for the next three months. Seeing Mitch with Brenda Timmins is just more than I can take." She looked out the window and said in a halting voice, "You were right, Mom. All of those things you tried to tell me were right."

Beth put her arm around Jimmy Lee's shoulders. "The last couple of months have been hard, haven't they?"

Jimmy Lee closed her eyes against the stabbing pain. "I really hate this, Mom."

Beth's arms tightened around her. "I know, honey. I know."

Jimmy Lee leaned against her mother wordlessly. Whoever said crying helped ease the pain had lied, she decided. She felt worse now than she had ever thought possible.

A few minutes later Jimmy Lee sat at the table, her eyes finally dry. Allison, her younger sister, walked through the door. "Hi," she said. "Everybody's heard about you and Mitch."

"How can that be?" Jimmy Lee asked. "You don't even go to high school."

"Merrilyn heard it from Mitch's younger brother," she said, cutting herself a piece of cake. "You know how news travels around Georgemont Junior High."

"Yeah, I know."

"Listen, Merrilyn wanted to know if you were going to keep the baseball cap he gave you."

"Why?"

"If you don't want it, she'd like to have it." Allison began to eat the cake in her hand.

Jimmy Lee set her jaw. "Vultures are already starting to hover."

"Jimmy Lee," Beth scolded gently.

"Well, Mom, that's rude!" Jimmy Lee countered. "I'm not going to give her my baseball cap. The last thing I need to see is Merrilyn Thornton running around our house with Mitch's baseball cap on." She faced Allison, blinking back tears. "How could you talk to Merrilyn about my breakup?"

Allison looked down. "I'm sorry," she said. "I didn't think it would bother you."

"Well, it does."

"That's enough, Jimmy Lee," Beth broke in. "You don't need to be taking your anger out on your sister. You can't expect people not to talk about the breakup. It's just the kind of thing people are interested in and they *will* talk about it. But Allison, you shouldn't be the one passing on details. Your sister is really hurting, and you need to show a little thoughtfulness and loyalty."

"I'm sorry, Jimmy Lee. I didn't know. Honest, I didn't. But people are going to ask me questions. What do you want me to say?" Allison asked.

"Just tell them that we wanted to go out with other people. Besides, it's really nobody's business, so you can tell them that, if you want to."

Allison smiled slyly. "I just might."

Jimmy Lee smiled wanly and stood up. Homework and evening chores still awaited. She picked up her books and trudged to her bedroom. Carefully, she sat on the bed and looked around. Everywhere she looked were pieces of her life with Mitch. The prom picture sat on her dresser, and photos of last year's triumph on the basketball court littered her walls. Mitch's dog, Ruff, frolicked with them in the snow. Happy grins lit faces in a group of photos pinned to her bulletin board.

Jimmy Lee shook her head. Last winter had been wonderful, with bright, snow-filled days. Both she and Mitch were experienced cross-country skiers, and many Saturday mornings, after those exhilarating and exhausting Friday night games, they would put their skis in the back of Mitch's father's pickup and head for the mountains. Ruff, a black, long-hair mixture of Irish setter and Labrador, always sat between them on the bench seat, wiggling with anticipation.

Carrying packs with hot chocolate, water, and sandwiches, they would park on the shoulder of the road and make their own trail into Oregon's Cascade range. Sometimes the days were noisy romps, sometimes awe-filled at the crystalline beauty and quiet serenity. Always the fact that they were sharing it together made their appreciation intimate and personal. Those days would end when, tired and invigorated at the same time, they would follow their trail back to the truck. Usually Ruff would flop down and put his head in Jimmy Lee's lap while Mitch drove. A comfortable silence would envelop the threesome. Mitch would quietly reach over, his arm on the back of the seat, and rub Jimmy Lee's neck, his warm fingers easing the tired muscles.

A knock sounded on her door. Clearing her throat, she hastily wiped her face with the back of her hand. "Come in."

Beth opened the door. "It's time for dinner, honey," she said.

Jimmy Lee wasn't hungry. She should just skip it. But looking at her mother's face, she read the quiet expectation. *You will not hide from this. You will not give in to this.* Jimmy Lee felt her heart rise to meet that expectation. "Okay," she said. "I'll wash my hands."

CHAPTER 4

Kody sat in anatomy class, impatiently jiggling his foot. His next class was chemistry and he was excited to see Jimmy Lee again. He couldn't believe she had chosen him to be her lab partner.

Then a new thought suddenly exploded. What if she had changed her mind? Maybe after the scene with Ken Mackley she'd decided Kody wasn't worth knowing because of his paralyzed embarrassment. What could he do? Should he think of an alternative partner? Maybe he should drop the class.

"Get a grip," he scolded himself. "If she's changed her mind she'll explain it in a civilized way, you'll respond in a civilized way."

Again, he was one of the first in the room. He sat down, anxiously waiting. Soon Jimmy Lee walked in quietly, dropped her books on the table, and sat down next to him. "Hi," she said.

Relief flooded through Kody. In spite of yesterday's experience, Jimmy Lee still would be his lab partner. He wondered how she was feeling about Mitch and was about to ask, then remembered how sympathy had made her feel the previous day. "How did your homework go?" he asked instead.

"Okay, I guess." She pulled out her class notes and assignment. "How about you?"

"I think I did all right on the essay question, but the equation was tough." Kody presented his own set of notes. Even before the bell rang they were absorbed in the preliminary science equation that would lead to their experiment in class.

After Mr. Bradley had called the class to order and given a short lecture on preparing the experiment, they returned to their studies and worked until the bell rang.

"This feels like the shortest class I've ever had," Kody said, waiting as Jimmy Lee gathered her books.

"I hope we'll have enough class time to prepare for our experiment," Jimmy Lee said.

"Oh, I think it'll be okay. We work well together."

"Yeah, we do," Jimmy Lee agreed. In the crowded hallway, she asked, "What did you do last night, besides homework?"

"Not much. Just worked on my homework and practiced my oboe. What about you?"

"Chores and homework. Reanna took me home. She always drives me to school and home again. It's real nice. That way we can have some time to talk every day. Do you know Reanna? She's my best friend."

"Yeah, I know her," Kody said. Who didn't know Reanna? She was one of the prettiest girls in the school. She and Kody had shared English class during the previous semester, and Kody had often found himself staring at the blonde-haired girl. Then he would turn away, embarrassed, hoping no one noticed. No one did.

Kody tried to think of an absorbing conversational topic to keep Jimmy Lee's mind occupied. He didn't want her to look for Mitch. But every few feet someone paused to say something sympathetic or pat her shoulder.

Jimmy Lee smiled and said, "Thanks," and "I'm fine." But she kept moving. It was obvious that she didn't want to get trapped into a conversation. Kody stuck faithfully beside her. Then he saw Reanna hurrying toward them. "Look, there's Reanna," he said, pointing at the blonde girl enthusiastically.

Jimmy Lee followed his gaze and smiled. "Sure enough," she said with relief. She stopped, waiting for her friend to catch up. "What's new?" she asked.

"I just wanted to remind you to bring some old clothes when you come over to my house on Friday. We're working at the stake center Saturday morning. We'll be finishing off the flower bed. Do you remember?" Reanna was bouncy and smiling.

"Oh, no. I'd forgotten. Good thing you reminded me." She glanced at Kody. "Kody, do you know Reanna?"

Kody could feel himself blushing. "Yes, but we've never formally met."

"Call me Reenie. Everybody does," said Reanna. "You're Kody McLaughlin from English class last semester, aren't you?"

Kody nodded, surprised and pleased.

"Hey, I have an idea. Why don't you join us on Saturday, Kody. We could use all the help we can get."

"Yeah. Why don't you?" Jimmy Lee chimed in. "Are you busy Saturday morning at ten?"

Kody blinked and cleared his throat. An invitation to spend time with these two popular girls caught him off guard. "No, I'm not busy, but . . . um, well, what exactly is a stake center?"

Reanna explained. "It's the church building on Alderwood Lane. It's the hub of the Mormons' activities in this area."

Kody knew the street. "The brick building with new landscaping?" he asked. "What will you be doing there?"

"We'll be pulling any weeds that have cropped up in the last little while, but mostly we'll be spreading bark dust and edging the flower beds with rocks," Jimmy Lee replied. "Last fall we planted a bunch of bulbs and we have to spread the dust before they begin to pop up."

The late bell rang. Reanna pursed her lips. "I wasn't even paying attention," she muttered in frustration. "Boy, am I going to get it. Mrs. Brighton is a real stickler about tardiness. Don't forget the clothes, Jimmy Lee," she said, and she broke into a run.

"We'd better hurry too," Jimmy Lee said.

In the Humanities building Jimmy Lee and Kody strode down the long hall, passing other latecomers scurrying for their class. As they turned the corner to their classroom they practically ran into Mitch and Brenda. Mitch was in a leisurely pose, leaning against the wall. Brenda was glued to him like wallpaper. When Mitch saw Jimmy Lee he straightened up, pushing away from the wall. Brenda turned her head and a languid smile spread across her face.

Mitch looked uncomfortable. He tugged at Brenda's hand. "C'mon Brenda, we've got to get you to class," he said in a low voice.

"Why, Mitch, what's your hurry?" Brenda drawled. "It's been so long since I've seen Jimmy Lee. We might be in the mood for a visit. You know, compare notes." She winked at Jimmy Lee.

Kody could feel the anger boiling inside of him. How could Brenda be so mean? "Brenda Timmins, you don't have the class to compare notes with Jimmy Lee." Kody began, surprised at hearing his own voice. "The only piece of Mitch you've been able to get is leftovers." Grabbing the stricken Jimmy Lee's hand, Kody deftly pulled her away, but not before he heard Brenda retort loudly, "What a runty little fur ball."

Kody ignored the comment and hurried Jimmy Lee around the next corner. When they were out of sight they stopped, looking at each other. "Kody, I'm surprised at you," Jimmy Lee said.

Kody blushed. "I'm surprised at me too," he said. "I'm sorry. I guess it's none of my business, but Brenda Timmins has all the appeal of a scorpion."

Jimmy Lee bit her lip and Kody was afraid she would start to cry. Instead, she giggled. She clapped her hand to her mouth, but the laughter spilled out. "Oh, Kody," she cried, sliding down the wall, still shaking with laughter. "Did you see the look on Brenda's face? It was priceless." Jimmy Lee puffed out her cheeks and crossed her eyes in an imitation of Brenda's shocked look, then doubled over again.

Kody grabbed her hand and pulled her up. "You'd better be quiet," he whispered. "Or we're going to get in trouble. We've already been docked five points in Mr. Sandival's class."

Jimmy Lee sobered, then giggled again. "I'm sorry," she said wiping her eyes. "I haven't had such a good laugh for a long time." She looked directly into his eyes and said seriously, "Thanks Kody. I don't know what I would've done if I'd been alone."

Kody felt warm all over at her praise. "Well, now we're even," he said. "You stood up to Ken Mackley yesterday when I didn't know what to say."

"Oh, Ken," shrugged Jimmy Lee. "He really is a bully, isn't he? I wonder why he grew up so mean."

They paused at the closed door of their sociology class. Jimmy Lee put her hand on the knob and winked at Kody. "Well, here goes."

As they listened to Mr. Sandival lecture them on the importance of punctuality and the five points to be docked from their final grade, Kody's face showed nothing but contrition, but he was making a decision. He would go with Jimmy Lee and Reanna to work at their church building. He had never known anyone like Jimmy Lee. Under those cowboy boots and flannel shirts was sensitivity, loyalty, and zest for life. How could somebody so tough and determined also be vulnerable and soft? The combination that would've been a contradiction in most people seemed to fit Jimmy Lee perfectly. Kody suddenly wanted, more than anything in the world, to be her friend.

Kody slipped into his place at the dining room table and took the steaming bowl of spaghetti his Mom handed him. "Mom, this looks great! My favorite!" he enthused.

Vonnie McLaughlin smiled. "I know how you feel about my spaghetti, and since this is your first week back at school after Christmas vacation I thought I'd make you something special."

Kody helped himself generously to the steaming pasta. "I wonder how Kyle and Christine are doing now that they're back at college?"

"I'm sure they're missing your mother's home cooking." Michael McLaughlin, Kody's father, already had his plate full.

Kody grinned. "No doubt about that." He thought about his brother and sister, both away at different universities. Kyle wasn't big, but he certainly was good-looking. His thick auburn hair had a natural curl that always fell into place. He also had the body of an athlete, even though he wasn't very tall. Christine was the beauty. Petite, with long strawberry-blond hair, peachy skin, and emerald green eyes, she had graduated from Pinecrest the previous year. Teachers who knew Christine did a double take the first time they read "McLaughlin" on the roll. Kody knew he didn't look anything like Christine—or Kyle, either.

Following in their footsteps was not easy, he had discovered. He saw disbelief in his teachers' eyes when he told them he was Christine McLaughlin's brother. Christine and Kody didn't even appear to be remotely related, much less brother and sister. But in spite of the obvious hardships Kody faced because of his older siblings, he loved them dearly. Now that they were at college he missed them. The McLaughlins were a tight-knit group. Kyle and Christine had always accepted him and never teased him about his size or his hair. During the Christmas break they had even attended his oboe recital. It would be a long time before they came home from college. Spring break was four months away, in April.

"So, Kody," asked his father, "how do you like your classes?"

"They're okay. A couple of them are real tough."

"I know you're taking calculus this semester. How is your homework coming along?"

Kody put his fork down. "Calculus is hard. I was hoping you could help me with it later."

"Sure. We'll take a look at it after dinner. How about third-year chemistry? Is that hard too?"

"Not so bad. I have a partner in chemistry, and she's pretty smart. Between the two of us we usually work stuff out."

"I didn't know you needed partners for chemistry," Vonnie said. "What's her name?"

"Lab partners," explained Kody, reaching for the Parmesan cheese. "Her name is Jimmy Lee Donovan."

"Jimmy Lee? Isn't that kind of a strange name for a girl?"

Kody put a forkful of spaghetti in his mouth and tried to talk. His mother gave him a stern look and Kody carefully chewed and swallowed before continuing. "I used to think that very thing, but now that I've gotten to know her I think it fits. She's really great, and like I said, she's smart. She wants to go to BYU after graduation, so she works hard in school."

"BYU," Michael McLaughlin mused. "Isn't that the big Mormon college in Utah?"

"Yeah."

"Is Jimmy Lee a Mormon?"

"Yeah. She's a Mormon, and her best friend, Reanna Lewis, is a Mormon too. Oh, that reminds me, they asked if I could go with them on Saturday to work on the grounds of the church."

Vonnie and Michael exchanged glances. "What will you be doing?" Vonnie asked.

"I guess they planted a bunch of bulbs last fall and they want to spread the bark dust and edge the planter with rocks before the bulbs pop up this spring."

"Is it the new building on Alderwood Lane?"

"Yeah. That's the one."

"Will there be any religious training?"

Kody blinked. "I don't know," he said. "They didn't mention it."

"They don't always," Michael said. He looked again at Vonnie. "What do you think?"

Vonnie spoke. "It's okay if you go, Kody, but if there's some religious discussion we'd like to hear about it."

"Okay."

"Also, we'd like to meet these girls. It sounds like you and Jimmy Lee are more than just lab partners."

"Oh, Mom, it's nothing like that. She's a lot of fun and I like being with her, but we don't feel romantic about each other. Actually, she just broke up with her boyfriend." Kody told his folks about Mitch and how he had tried to help Jimmy Lee during the past week of school. "I think she's feeling better."

"I have no doubt, Kody," Michael said. "You're a good friend. I have an idea. Why don't you bring the girls home after you're finished working this Saturday? Your mother could make a big pot of soup and you could watch some videos."

Vonnie shook her head. "I won't be home this Saturday. I'm going to Ashland for that computer seminar. Remember?"

"Oh, right. How about next Saturday?"

Kody was enthusiastic. "It sounds good to me. I'll ask the girls and see if they can come over. You'll like them."

He turned his attention to his meal. What was this about a religious class? His folks sounded pretty ominous. What might they know? And what did Mormons believe, anyway? His parents never talked about religion, and nobody in the family went to church. Were they worried about Jimmy Lee and Reanna being Mormons?

Vonnie interrupted his thoughts. "How is your oboe practice coming along?"

Kody swallowed another mouthful, then answered, "Okay, I guess."

His heart began to beat heavily. The last few practices had been dismal affairs. It was always hard to get his lungs back in shape after taking time off. But the time off had been wonderful. For two full weeks he hadn't worried about his oboe. The only time during the year when he didn't have to practice or go to his weekly lessons was after his Christmas recital. Instead he watched the college bowl games on television and ate popcorn and potato chips.

No one in school, except the music teacher and the players in the band, knew he could play the oboe. It wasn't an ability of which Kody was particularly proud. Ever since sixth grade he had been able to play the instrument well, but what he really wanted to play was sports. He loved team games, but his body build doomed him to observer status.

This was especially frustrating during football season. As part of the band, he had to march with the rest of the instrument-toting students during half-time. During the game he would sit with the band in the far corner of the bleachers and watch the football team run around the field while the crowd cheered. During these games, envy and disappointment pushed out any music in his heart. Kody especially hated the drills every first period on the soggy football field's turf. It was a daily reminder of what he never would be able to accomplish.

Most of the band music was easy and didn't take any practicing. It was classical music that Kody worked on during his home practice sessions. Bach, Mozart, and other composers from both the past and the modern day kept him glued to the notes until he understood the music. Still, it wasn't what he hoped to be doing; and even after playing a difficult piece Kody never really triumphed. Sometimes he wondered why he practiced at all. Then he would remember the encouragement of his parents and his music teacher, Mr. Svenson: his oboe might be the ticket to a music scholarship that would open the doors into one of the finer colleges.

Vonnie continued. "I know Mr. Svenson will be pleased to start your lessons again, since you've had Christmas break off. Do you think you'll be ready next week?"

"It'll be fine," he said. "It won't take me long to get back into shape."

"I hope not," Vonnie said. "You'll have to start working on the music you want to use for your scholarship presentations next year."

Kody nodded but dreaded the thought of the work before him. Colleges from all over the nation would want a video presentation of him playing his oboe. He would have to select at least four different pieces from the different eras of music, and those four pieces would have to showcase his ability. It was a daunting task and one that didn't encourage his enthusiasm.

Sighing, Kody chased down the last lettuce leaf. "Thanks for dinner, Mom. It was great."

Vonnie smiled. "You're welcome, Kody. I'm looking forward to hearing you practice."

Kody nodded and put his plate in the sink.

CHAPTER 5

On Friday evening Jimmy Lee sat with Reanna in the Lewises family room, dipping abstractedly into the bowl of popcorn between them. The videos were stacked forgotten on the coffee table as Jimmy Lee talked. She told Reanna about the surprise meeting with Mitch and Brenda in the hallway. They'd laughed, but then melancholy set in once again. The thought of Brenda plastered to Mitch like that, and Mitch, posing like a clothes ad—it was awful. The only bright spot had been Kody's quick defense. "You should've seen the way he flew at Brenda," Jimmy Lee chuckled.

Reanna smiled. "Now, there's a real friend. Standing up to Mitch and Brenda wouldn't be easy."

Jimmy Lee looked at her hands. "You know, Reenie, if Mitch called me this instant and asked me to take him back, I'd do it."

Reanna's eyes grew large. "You would? Even after all of this?"

Jimmy Lee nodded. "I'd do it in a heartbeat."

Reanna gnawed her lip, then spoke decisively. "To tell you the truth, Jimmy Lee, I'm sorry I ever set the two of you up, and I'm glad the two of you broke up."

Jimmy Lee stared at her, shocked. "How can you say such a thing?" she asked.

"Think about it," Reanna began. "I've seen you and talked with you more on the phone these last few days than all of December! I mean, you never had any time for me. I never even saw you during the study hall we have together. You always used to get a hall pass so you could spend the time with Mitch."

Jimmy Lee was silent. "I never thought of it that way," she finally said.

"You know, it doesn't surprise me that the Church discourages long-term relationships at our age. Personally, I don't think it's healthy. I mean, the two of you were so close there wasn't any room for anyone else."

"I'm sorry, Reenie. I never meant to exclude you. Honest, I didn't."

"I know," Reanna said. "And I'm not trying to make you feel bad. It's just that—well, I thought I owed you my true opinion. And I'll give you some advice too: start dating."

"What?" Jimmy Lee sat up straight. "Start dating! You've got to be kidding. We haven't even been apart a week."

"A week, a month. What's the difference? You need to start finding out that there are other guys in this world besides Mitch. How long did he wait?"

"That's easy for you to say, Reenie. You've always liked seeing someone new every weekend. That's never been my style, and I'm certainly not going to begin now."

"How do you know it's not your style?" Reanna retorted. "You've never given it a chance."

Jimmy Lee couldn't argue about that. She'd started dating Mitch the same month she turned sixteen. She'd literally never dated anyone else. What would it be like to see someone else? Where could she even start? Who would ask her out? Besides, she never considered herself the dating type. Not like Reanna, with her blonde hair and long lashes. Boys were just automatically attracted to her. Why, even Kody blushed and acted silly when he was introduced to her.

"I'm sorry," Reanna was saying. "I didn't mean to hurt your feelings."

Jimmy Lee blinked. "You didn't hurt my feelings. You were just being honest." She paused. "It's just that I'm not real sure where to go from here, Reenie. I mean, what's next? And don't tell me to date every guy at school. I really don't want to do that."

"Do you want to double date with me?" Reanna asked hopefully. "I could—"

Jimmy Lee shrieked. "No! Weren't you just apologizing thirty seconds ago for lining me up with Mitch?" She smacked Reanna with a cushion and they both burst out laughing.

"Okay, okay," huffed Reanna. "I can take a hint. So, just concentrate on good friends right now. That's a good place to start. You've got me, and Kody McLaughlin has been a real sweetie."

Jimmy Lee smiled. "Well, he certainly showed his colors today."

"I'm glad he decided to work with us tomorrow. We may not have very many show up."

"What makes you say that?" Jimmy Lee asked.

"No food," Reanna giggled. Then she yawned. "What do you say we watch one of these movies before we hit the sack?"

On Saturday morning Kody woke late and hurried through his shower and dressing. When he looked in the mirror he saw that his flannel shirt was wrinkled and his socks didn't match. He switched to a navy sweatshirt. Better. Pulling off the black sock, Kody dug around until he found the match to the blue one he was wearing. Then he laced up his shoes and quietly walked to the living room window. His mother had left for Ashland a couple of hours ago but Kody's dad was still sleeping.

In the kitchen Kody made himself a stack of toast and slathered on the butter and jam. While he ate, he wrote a note for his father: "See you around one this afternoon."

He finished the toast at the living room window, then slipped out when he saw Reanna's car. He climbed in the back seat after Jimmy Lee leaned back to open the door. "My mom left for Ashland a while ago," he announced. "She's got some computer class she's taking, and my dad is still asleep. I left a note saying I'd be back around one this afternoon. Is that right?"

"Perfect," Jimmy Lee said.

Reanna put the car in gear and glanced at Kody in the rearview mirror. "Some people you'll know from school, but our stake includes Eagleridge High too. So you won't know everybody."

Kody asked the question that was on his mind. "Will there be some religious teaching today?"

Reanna and Jimmy Lee exchanged quick glances. "No," Jimmy Lee said. "Why?"

Kody shrugged. "My folks wanted to know."

"Did they have reservations about letting you come with us today?" Reanna asked.

"Not at all," Kody replied. It was difficult to take his eyes off the mirror. Reanna was definitely the prettiest girl in the whole school. It was hard to picture her working in the dirt.

When they arrived at the church, Kody knew he was right about Reanna. She stood next to a wheelbarrow full of bark dust looking dubiously at the shovel propped against it. He grinned. Reanna gave the impression that she was waiting for the wooden chips to spread themselves. She was dressed in petite jeans and an oversized white sweater. Even her canvas shoes were white.

Jimmy Lee's reaction was just the opposite. She picked up the handles of the wheelbarrow, shoved it to an open section of the bed, and began shoveling the wood chips over the earth in long, even sweeps. Her lips were compressed into a thin line. Kody didn't have to guess what she was thinking every time she stabbed the mound of bark dust with her shovel.

Soon he was beside her with his own tools. "What are you thinking?" he asked.

Jimmy Lee gave him a quick glance before returning to her work. "Last fall when we planted these bulbs I asked Mitch if he would come and help, but he said no. Something about an early basketball practice." She stabbed the mound again.

"Do you think he lied?" Kody asked bluntly as he began working.

"Oh, I don't know," Jimmy Lee replied with disgust. After a few minutes of silent work, her mood changed. She stopped and wiped her sweating forehead. "Come spring, all of this will be in bloom," she said as she swept her hand over the flower beds. "Crocus, daffodils, tulips, iris, hyacinth, lilies. You name it."

Kody had passed the church many times and couldn't remember seeing flowers in bloom before. He tried to picture the sea of color that the March and April sunshine would nurture into life. "Are they all new?" he asked.

"Yes, and I can't wait for them to bloom," Jimmy Lee said as she went back to work. "I love flowers."

Soon they were joined by Joseph Sumpter and Scott Pearson. Kody knew them vaguely from school.

"Hi, Jimmy Lee, Hi Kody," both boys said in unison. Joseph asked, "Kody, would you mind helping us move that pile of gravel?" He pointed to a nearby mound.

Kody shouldered his shovel. "I'll be right back," he said to Jimmy Lee.

The three boys moved off, but Jimmy Lee called after them. "Don't let these two rope you into doing all of the work," she warned.

The three boys grinned at one another and began shoveling the gravel into the empty wheelbarrows. Kody saw others who looked familiar from school, but he didn't know all of them. One boy, who looked unfamiliar, was talking to Reanna. He was leaning on his shovel and gazing intently into her eyes as they spoke. Their conversation looked private, and Kody felt a stab of jealousy. He turned away from the couple and tried to concentrate on his work and the two boys beside him. Joseph and Scott. Kody didn't know either very well, but Joseph had been in the band for a short time.

"Why did you quit band?" Kody asked.

Joseph shrugged. "I never was very good," he said. "Not like you."

The comment was casual, but Kody was taken by surprise. He didn't know anyone paid any attention when he played.

Joseph continued: "I remember one day last year, before I quit. We had just finished marching for the season and I was sitting behind you in class. I looked over your shoulder and noticed you fingering out an oboe concerto by Mozart. You were practicing before the band teacher came in." Joseph laughed. "I couldn't play Mozart to save my life."

"But you don't play the oboe," Kody said. "You played the saxophone. Mozart never wrote anything for the saxophone."

Joseph laughed. "Yeah, but the trouble was, I couldn't play anything written for the saxophone, either."

"Hey, will you two get to work? I'm the only one who's putting any muscle into this," Scott teased.

"Actually, I like that arrangement," Joseph retorted with a sly smile.

Kody grinned at Joseph and stabbed the mound with his shovel. Once again, he glanced at Reanna. The young man was still beside her. They were both working, but with little enthusiasm. They seemed to be more interested in each other. Kody turned away. "This will look nice when it's all finished," he said.

Joseph nodded in agreement, and all three boys turned their full attention to their work. Every now and then Kody would hear his name being called and he would look up to greet someone. Mark and Jason from the football team were there. Were they Mormons?

"Hey, Kody," Jason said easily. "Jimmy Lee said you'd be coming today, but we didn't believe her."

"Why not?" Kody asked.

"Because there isn't any food," Mark responded. "I'm surprised *we're* here."

Both boys laughed and Kody smiled. It felt good to be included.

After the boys moved the gravel, Kody returned to Jimmy

Lee's side and worked in silence, thinking. These kids were different than any of the other people he knew from school. Their speech was different. They respected and accepted each other. Just the fact that they were spending their Saturday morning working on church grounds proved they were different. And they all seemed confident and strong. Even Jimmy Lee, who was suffering, had a core of strength that seemed to come from inside. He had quaked before Ken Mackley, yet Jimmy Lee showed no fear. Where did it come from? Did it come from being a Mormon? Some kids at school made fun of Jimmy Lee, Reanna, and the other Mormons—like Ken Mackley. Other kids thought religion was some sort of a crutch for people who weren't strong enough to make it on their own. But when Kody looked at Reanna and Jimmy Lee he didn't see weakness. He saw strength, and it didn't come from something as temporary as a crutch.

Kody didn't even know if there was a God. Religion was simply not a part of his home.

Jimmy Lee placed her gloved hand on his arm. "Make sure you don't hit any of the bulbs," she said.

Seeing that his hoe was making gouges, Kody stopped, panting. "Oh, I guess I'm getting a little carried away," he said.

Jimmy Lee was quick to smile. "Maybe you can make up for Reenie's lack of enthusiasm."

Kody glanced at Reanna. The young man beside her was grinning.

Reanna ignored Jimmy Lee's teasing barb and made a brief introduction. "Kody, this is Eric Miller. He goes to school at Eagleridge High."

"Hi."

"Hi, Kody." Eric smiled easily.

Kody found it hard not to like him in spite of the jealousy he had felt earlier. He tried to put that away and concentrate on his work.

Jimmy Lee turned to Reanna. "Hurry, Reenie. If you had half of the energy Kody has, we'd be finished in no time."

Reanna pouted. "It's cold out and I forgot my work gloves."

"Since when have you owned a pair of work gloves?" Jimmy Lee asked.

"Here, use these." Kody removed his gloves and walked to where Reanna was standing in the dirt. "I'll be fine." He glanced at Eric and noticed that he didn't have any work gloves either.

"Are you sure?" Reanna asked.

Kody nodded. "If you hurry, they might still be warm."

Reanna quickly slipped the gloves on and breathed a sigh of relief. "Thanks, Kody."

"Now you don't have any excuses, Reenie," Jimmy Lee gibed. "If you work a little, the rest of you will get warm, too."

"Well, you're just full of advice, aren't you, Jimmy Lee?" Reanna mock-sulked.

Jimmy Lee turned to Kody. "We were going to go out for pizza afterwards. Can you come along?" she asked.

Kody hesitated. "As long as I'm home by one, I think it'll be okay, but I probably should change my clothes first."

"Naw. Don't worry about that. I'm not going to change. We'll just send Reenie to the counter for our order. She's the cleanest."

"Eric, will you be coming along?" Kody asked.

Eric shook his head. "I've got to go to work this afternoon."

Kody felt happier. He turned to Reanna and asked, "Where did you get your nickname?"

Reanna looked slyly at Jimmy Lee. "If I tell my story, you've got to tell yours."

Jimmy Lee made a face. "That's not fair," she said. "Reanna is much easier to live with than my full name."

"So, is Jimmy Lee a nickname?" Kody asked.

Just then Jimmy Lee's dad walked up, a younger girl holding his hand. Kody had heard the kids calling him President Donovan, and he wondered why.

"I don't think I've met your friend, Jimmy Lee."

Jimmy Lee performed the introductions and Kody shook hands with her father and said hello to her younger sister, Allison. Kody was impressed with the father's firm handshake and warm, open smile.

"Glad you could make it. How do you know Jimmy Lee?" Wes Donovan asked.

"We're partners in chemistry and we have sociology together," Kody explained.

"He keeps me focused on my work," Jimmy Lee said. "So I don't think about Mitch quite so much."

"Ah, Mitch." Wes Donovan turned to Kody. "Jimmy Lee told me about the way you rescued her in the hallway. She says she was positively tongue-tied and you saved the day."

Kody was pleased. It made him feel good to know Jimmy Lee thought about him after school. "Did she tell you about how she stood up for me? Ken Mackley was being a real jerk and Jimmy Lee gave him a piece of her mind."

Wes Donovan laughed and put his arm around Jimmy Lee. "No one ever accused Jimmy Lee of being shy. She doesn't mind voicing her opinion when someone is behaving badly."

Jimmy Lee hugged her father. "I wonder who I got that from?" she asked.

"Probably from your mother," her father responded. "She's been known to quell a family uprising a time or two. See you at home, Jimmy Lee."

"Don't forget we're going out for pizza afterwards," Jimmy Lee called after him. Wes Donovan waved as he walked away with Allison.

"Why does everybody call your dad President Donovan?" Kody asked Jimmy Lee.

"He's the stake president," Jimmy Lee explained. "He presides over the Church members in this area."

Kody nodded, but he really didn't understand.

It didn't seem long before the work was finished. Kody looked around. The grounds definitely looked tidy and trim, the beds waiting for warmer weather to call the bulbs to life without competition from weeds or grass. "It looks great," Kody said with admiration.

"Wait until spring," Jimmy Lee replied, then added musingly, as if to herself, "How do the flowers know it's time to bloom? All that beauty, setting itself according to the clock of nature."

Before Kody could answer, Wes Donovan was speaking. He thanked everyone for coming and asked Scott to give a closing prayer. Caught off guard, Kody awkwardly imitated Jimmy Lee by folding his arms, bowing his head, and closing his eyes. Scott seemed to know just what to say to God, he thought. And no questions about whether He existed.

Over pizza, he cocked an eye at Jimmy Lee. "So, how exactly did you get your nickname?" he asked.

"Out with the story," Reanna teased.

Jimmy Lee sighed. "My mother had a favorite aunt named Genamina," she began. "She never married, but my mother promised she would name her first daughter after her. My dad didn't care for the name at all, and started calling me Jimmy Lee. It just kind of stuck."

"Why not Jenny? Or Mina? They seem like the natural choices," Kody asked

Reanna shook her head. "Does she look like a Jenny to you?"

Kody had to submit to Reanna's logic. "No. And she doesn't look like a Genamina either."

"She hates Genamina," confided Reanna. "Don't you, Jimmy Lee? Whenever we start a new semester, she asks each teacher before class to call her Jimmy Lee when they're calling roll. So far no one has forgotten and very few people at school know her real name."

"I think that's enough about *my* past, Reanna," Jimmy Lee said. "It's your turn now."

"When I was born, my older brother, Byron, couldn't pronounce Reanna. He called me Reenie. Not very exciting," Reanna bit into a fresh piece of pizza.

Kody wished he had an interesting story to tell, but he didn't. He was just plain old Kody—no nicknames, no secrets.

CHAPTER 6

At the supper table that night Kody surveyed the chicken enchiladas his father was dishing up. "Dad, this is great!" he enthused. "I didn't know you could make chicken enchiladas."

"That's because I never have," Michael said. "But with your mother getting home just in time for dinner, I figured I ought to do the cooking. I just followed the recipe. It wasn't all that hard, but it was messy."

Kody looked into the kitchen. His father must have used every pot, plate, and casserole dish in the house.

"Don't worry," Vonnie said. "It smells wonderful, and we'll all pitch in and help clean up."

"How did your class go, Mom?" Kody asked.

"It was very interesting. I wish you could've been there. I think you would've enjoyed it. The teacher talked a lot about the Internet. Computers are changing so fast that I could probably take this same seminar next year and it would be completely different. This will really help me at the office, though. The insurance business is beginning to rely on computers for a lot of tasks and I don't want to be left behind."

"How did your morning go with Jimmy Lee and Reanna?" Michael asked.

"Good. It was fun."

"Fun? Since when is yard work fun?" Vonnie asked.

Kody was thoughtful. "It wasn't that hard, because there were so many people helping out; and it was nice to spend some time with Jimmy Lee and Reanna."

"Was there a religious meeting?"

"No. Just yard work. Reanna, Jimmy Lee, and I went out for a pizza afterwards but we never discussed religion. It did make me wonder, though."

"About what?" Michael asked.

"I don't know, exactly. I didn't know all of these kids—just a few from school, and they're great. But it's more than that. They seem to be"—he searched for the right word—"connected somehow. And they all seem strong and confident." He became frustrated. "I'm not explaining this very well. I guess I just wished I understood more about their religion."

"Do you find it intriguing?" Vonnie asked.

"Yeah. I guess that's the right word. It's intriguing."

"I've never found churches all that intriguing," Michael said. "Christianity is mostly a business these days."

"It doesn't seem like a business," Kody said.

"There's a lot of money wrapped up in religion. Just look at all those people on TV, willing to sell you something they don't even own. Salvation. To me that's a business. And not a very reputable one."

"Do you think Mormons are the same?"

"I'm sure they have ways of collecting funds. They might not broadcast it like some of these other people, but I bet if you were to look deep enough you'd find money playing a big part in their religion."

Kody nodded thoughtfully. Then he asked. "What do you believe, Mom? Do you think there's a God?"

Vonnie looked taken aback. "Well, Kody," she started. "I can't say either way. I guess I believe in a supreme being, but I don't think you need to go to church to worship. Have the girls asked you to attend any of their meetings?" Her hands moved nervously, pushing her fork through her enchiladas.

"No."

"If they do ask, what would you say?" she asked.

"I don't know. I haven't thought about it. I *am* interested in who they are. They're so different from the other kids at school."

"How?"

"Well, they don't drink, smoke, or party like a lot of the other kids, and the reason Mitch broke up with Jimmy Lee was because she wouldn't sleep with him."

"Is Mitch a Mormon?"

"No."

Michael stroked his chin. "I see. So what you're saying is that they have good, solid values."

"Yeah."

"But Kody, we have those values in this house too."

"I know, Dad, but so do a lot of other families and their kids still drink and carouse around. They just do it behind their parents' back."

"I'd like to meet these girls. Did you talk to them about coming over next Saturday?"

"Oh, no. I forgot, but I'll talk to them on Monday."

"Good enough," Vonnie said as she finished her meal. Then she changed the subject. "These enchiladas are great, Michael. I think the McLaughlin home has found a new cook."

Michael rose from the table. "Oh, no. I have a whole new respect for what you do, Vonnie. You could've whipped up this meal in half the time and with half the mess. Trust me, you don't want me to do this too often."

Vonnie smiled as she followed her husband into the kitchen. "What do ya say, Kody. Should we hire your father?"

"Sure, except next Saturday when the girls come over, I'd like you to make your chicken noodle soup, Mom. Would you mind?"

"Not at all."

A few minutes later, after Kody had finished helping in the kitchen, he went to his bedroom. In there, he was surrounded by pictures of great athletes. Michael Jordan hung on his closet door. Ken Griffey Jr. was smiling from the far wall, and a team picture of the San Francisco 49ers hung above the bed. This poster was his favorite. It was long, almost the length of his wall, and the team was dressed in their uniforms.

San Francisco was Kody's favorite team, and he knew not only the names of the players but also most of their stats by heart. He could recite the team record in his sleep, and he was looking forward to another Super Bowl with the 49ers in control.

Glancing away from his posters, he began putting his oboe together. Carefully he looked over the reed. He would have to make a new one soon. An endless and thankless task.

His mind wandered back over the day at the church. No one had done anything to exclude him. In fact, he had felt very included. But he could tell that the other young people had a bond deeper than friendship. Was it the Mormon God? Scott prayed as easily as he'd talked to Kody and Joseph. Was there really a God? Neither Reanna nor Jimmy Lee seemed to question it. Were churches really just trying to get money?

He wanted to know more, but he was afraid of asking Jimmy Lee and Reanna. They'd think he was a klutz or rude. Besides, they would never understand his fear. Their courage was one of the traits that drew him to them. Jimmy Lee had told Mitch no. How much courage had that taken? Knowing she might lose him to someone like Brenda? She was enduring a lot of pain now, but even though she was grieving she seemed to accept that life would go on. And she'd stood up to Ken Mackley. That took courage and strength. The very traits Kody knew *he* didn't have. He couldn't even ask Reanna or Jimmy Lee about their religion. What if there was a God? Did he even want to know? Suppose the answer was yes? What would his parents think? Almost certainly they'd be angry with him.

For the first time since starting high school, Kody really felt as if he was beginning to belong somewhere—not just in the band, but in a circle of friends.

The ring of the telephone caught his attention. He had been absently fitting the reed. Now he hastily finished. Just then his father called. "I'm not hearing your oboe."

Kody glanced up at the smiling athletes on his wall before playing a few notes. "Just getting started," he said.

* * *

The following Monday afternoon Kody sat in the living room of his oboe teacher, Mr. Svenson, waiting for his lesson. He was thinking about chemistry class. Once again, he had forgotten to ask Jimmy Lee and Reanna if they could come over Saturday afternoon. Tomorrow for sure. Through the closed door he could hear the other student wrestle with a piece of music Kody had mastered years ago. Sighing, Kody assembled his instrument and began quietly warming up.

As he did so, he recalled those earlier years of music. He had begun band in the fifth grade and private lessons in the sixth. He'd been enthusiastic, practicing two hours a day sometimes. He remembered his last band concert of grammar school. They had played at the expansive community college auditorium, with its cushioned seats and hardwood floor stage. Kody's heart had pounded with excitement when the first note vibrated in the big hall.

Soon came the special moment—his solo. Dressed in a black suit and bow tie his parents had bought him for this special occasion, Kody walked up to the microphone; and with his band teacher playing the piano accompaniment, he played a simple Bach piece. He smiled at the memory. He hadn't been even a tiny bit nervous. Excitement had been the only emotion rushing through him that evening. It had all come so naturally and easily, and it had been fun.

After his solo, Kody bowed to the applause and tried to locate his family. But the bright lights made the audience nothing but shadowy shapes sitting in chairs. He knew his family was out there. They were probably the small group in the middle who were standing as they clapped. It had been a glorious moment.

Mr. Svenson was in the audience that night, and after the concert he approached Kody and his parents and offered to tutor the blossoming musician. His credentials were noteworthy. He had toured the world with the New York Philharmonic in his earlier days, and his latest post had been that of the principal oboist at Portland Symphony. He had wanted to leave the east coast and move back to his native Pacific roots. Then he retired to Madrone, Oregon, where he taught students who had talent and a good work ethic. And Kody worked hard to please him.

Kody remembered well his first two lessons with Mr. Svenson. He had been more nervous about sitting next to the accomplished man than he had been about playing in front of the crowd at the auditorium. But on that first lesson Mr. Svenson did not play. Nor did Kody play. Instead Mr. Svenson taught him how to shave his own reeds. Turning them over in his hands and using precise but gentle motions, Mr. Svenson cut pieces of the bamboo until he was satisfied. Then he gave the reed to his student and Kody put it in his instrument under Mr. Svenson's careful eye.

Kody's first attempts at reed making were uncoordinated and sloppy, but Mr. Svenson praised his efforts and assigned practice time so that his reeds would someday look and sound as good as his teacher's.

That was in the distant past now. Somewhere along the way Kody's enthusiasm had gotten lost—the desire to please, the studious concentration on reeds and music, were gone. Kody's work ethic was now forced, and his ability to play hung only on his past effort. He made very little progress.

The music in the next room stopped. Mr. Svenson's patient voice explained something. Once again the playing began, and Kody could hear an improvement. Mr. Svenson was a good teacher. Kody knew he should appreciate the old man's efforts more—that and the money his parents were dishing out for his lessons. The music stopped and shortly a sixth-grade student came out.

Kody smiled. "The second time was better," he said.

The young girl smiled back. "You think so?"

"Yes, I do," Kody replied.

"Kody, you can come in now," Mr. Svenson said.

Kody hurried into the all-too-familiar studio. A baby grand

piano and an upholstered stool sat in one corner. Bookcases held sheaves of neatly organized music. There were enough chairs and stands for a quintet. A worn sofa stood against the wall, a stack of music magazines on one arm.

Mr. Svenson was thin and balding with fierce eyebrows and a graying beard. He motioned to the straight-backed chair next to his. "Let's get started," he said in his usual patient tone. "I'm running late today and I want to spend some extra time on the Mozart piece."

Kody put the reed to his lips and began the ambitious piece of music.

After he was finished, Mr. Svenson leaned back in his chair and sadly shook his head. "How many times must I tell you? Find joy in your playing. Technically you're correct. But musically it's a disaster. It's so vertical. There's no shape to the phrase. There's no joy." He looked anxiously into Kody's eyes. "You play well, but there is no warmth in the notes. I can't teach you warmth and a joy for playing." He seized Kody's knee and waggled it for emphasis as he exclaimed, "And until you learn those things you won't progress!"

Kody was taken aback. In five years Mr. Svenson had never before raised his voice. Every week he would patiently tell Kody he needed to not only play the notes but also interpret the music with warmth and sensitivity. What did those words mean anyway? Knowing his passages were correct, Kody had always dismissed the old man's notions.

Mr. Svenson continued. "Kody, I know I'm only your music teacher, but why don't you tell me what's going on in your life?"

"Nothing. I mean nothing is happening. Everything is fine."

"Okay, so nothing bad is happening. Is anything good happening?"

Kody thought for a moment. "Well, yes. I've made some new friends."

"Tell me about them."

"Two girls. They're a lot of fun and we've been spending some time together."

Mr. Svenson nodded. "What are their names?"

"Jimmy Lee Donovan and Reanna Lewis. Jimmy Lee is a strange name for a girl, but it fits her perfectly and she prefers it."

"That's wonderful, Kody. Now, I want you to play that friendship for me."

Kody blinked. "What do you mean?"

"As you were telling me about these two girls, your eyes came alive and you spoke with warmth and a smile. I want you to infuse your warm thoughts and feelings for these two girls into this Mozart concerto. When you play, think of your new friends."

"I . . . I . . ."

"No more questions. Just do it."

Kody took a deep breath and studied the music before playing. Then he played his first few notes. His notes turned into phrases and his phrases into passages. It was hard to think of Jimmy Lee and Reanna when he should be thinking of notes and breathing. He made mistakes but Mr. Svenson did not correct him. When he had finished the first movement, Mr. Svenson smiled. "What did you feel, Kody?"

Kody thought hard. "I felt like I was expressing something . . . I can't explain it."

"Indeed you were expressing something, and it showed through your music."

"What was I expressing?" Kody asked.

Mr. Svenson shook his head. "That's not for me to say. When you fine-tune that thought you'll find that your music is fine-tuned as well. Only then can you play in front of an audience and make them *feel* the music. Not just hear the music."

"But I made a lot of mistakes."

"Yes. Right now, you're used to thinking of your music as something separate from yourself and your feelings. It'll take time for you to infuse it into your life again and make it an integral part of your feelings. But the mistakes will lessen as you go."

"So do you want me to think of my friends from now on when I practice?"

Mr. Svenson thought for a moment, then answered. "Yes. Continue with the Mozart, and start working on the Haydn piece as well."

An hour later, Kody was in his own bedroom. He needed to practice, but all the warm feelings he had felt in Mr. Svenson's studio had dissipated. It was hard to think about playing the oboe when he was surrounded by smiling faces and brawny bodies who held baseball bats and footballs. Slowly Kody put his instrument together and began his warm-up notes. The sound seemed to be absorbed by the posters that hung on the wall, making his notes fall dead. In frustration, he quit playing and gazed at the posters. He would gladly give up his oboe if he could only toss a football like Joe Montana or Steve Young. He would be happy with making the Pinecrest High team. But even that was a joke.

Turning away from his wall, Kody tried to concentrate on the music on his stand, but every time he glanced up his thoughts were invaded by sports heroes. Maybe he needed to play in another room. Picking up his stand and oboe, he moved next door to Christine's old room. Her walls were covered in a floral print wallpaper that made it easier to think of the two girls. Well, Reanna at least. Kody doubted that Jimmy Lee would choose a floral print for her walls.

Setting the stand down, Kody began to play once again. He closed his eyes and tried to picture his two friends. Then he would make a mistake and his eyes would be forced open so that he could study the music. After thirty minutes he gave up. The only thing he was expressing was frustration. Mozart would have been infuriated. Heaving a heavy sigh, Kody picked up his stand and tromped back to his room.

CHAPTER 7

The following day Kody mouthed different versions of his invitation to Jimmy Lee on the way to chemistry. When she finally came in and sat next to him, he forgot them all and blurted out, "Would you like to come to my house this Saturday?"

Jimmy Lee looked startled. "Why, Kody, are you asking me for a date?"

Kody's eyes grew large and he shook his head vehemently. "No, nothing like that. I mean you and Reanna. My folks have mentioned they'd like to meet you, and I thought maybe we could play some basketball in the driveway or maybe watch a video."

Jimmy Lee smiled, at ease again. "Well, I can't speak for Reanna. She has a pretty full schedule, but I think it sounds like fun. I'd like to meet your parents."

After class, Kody and Jimmy Lee ran into Reanna, who was on her way to Mrs. Brighton's class.

"Kody has invited us to spend Saturday afternoon at his house," Jimmy Lee said. "Can you make it?"

Reanna pursed her lips. "Sure," she said. "What time?"

"Oh, I don't know," Kody said helplessly. "How about three-thirty? My mom said she'd make a big pot of soup, so we could eat an early dinner and watch a video after the basketball game."

Both girls nodded in agreement. "Sounds fun," exclaimed Reanna. "Thanks!"

Jimmy Lee and Kody were almost at their sociology classroom when Jimmy Lee stopped dead. "There's Mitch and Brenda," she said quietly, her voice laced with anger.

Kody followed Jimmy Lee's gaze. "Mitch doesn't look too happy," Kody commented casually.

"What do you mean?"

Kody shrugged as they began to move toward sociology once again. "I don't know. He just doesn't look"—he paused—"glad to have Brenda hanging all over him."

Jimmy Lee stopped walking and looked back. Could Kody be right? It was too late to tell. The couple were moving away, and all Jimmy Lee could see of him was his back. Brenda was wearing his coat. No, Kody was wrong. Mitch didn't look unhappy, just cold. "Thanks, Kody," she said with genuine appreciation before they hurried into sociology.

Kody heard the lecture with only half an ear. Both Jimmy Lee and Reanna had accepted his invitation! Not bad for a redheaded runt.

The following Saturday, by three-thirty Kody was so nervous that he finally went to his room. What if something went wrong? No. Something was certainly going to go wrong. The only question was what. "If there is a God, I hope you're watching this house." What Kody really hoped was that the subject of religion wouldn't come up. He didn't want his dad asking any embarrassing questions about Mormon finances.

"They're just driving up, Kody," Vonnie called.

Kody lunged out of his room toward the front door. The whole house was cozy with the aroma of chicken soup and rolls. He yanked the door open just as Jimmy Lee and Reanna came up the walk. Suddenly all his worries vanished. Just when anxiety should have been his strongest feeling, he felt completely relaxed. These girls were his friends. He liked them very much and they liked him. That's really all that mattered. Once they got to know them his parents wouldn't care what religion they belonged to.

"Hi, Kody," Jimmy Lee called, and tossed him the basketball she'd been holding. "I'm glad you've got a big driveway."

"There's plenty of room," Kody said. "Come meet my folks."

Kody couldn't stop grinning as he performed introductions, and they walked to the side door on waves of laughter and compliments about the soup smells.

"Our appetites are never very far away," Jimmy Lee grinned.

Outside, Kody noticed the sparkling sunshine for the first time. It had been gray and cloudy for weeks. Now the rain-scrubbed sky was azure blue. Light spilled everywhere. The chilly January breeze was light and the air felt good.

"Dad's agreed to give us the benefit of his experience," he said, "so the first order of business is to select teams."

"I'm not playing," Reanna said. "I just came to watch. No one told me this game wasn't on television."

Jimmy Lee rolled her eyes. "Reenie Lewis, you have to play."

"What if I break a fingernail?"

"The teams won't be even if you don't play."

Reanna looked around at the unsympathetic faces. Michael McLaughlin's mouth was twitching. "Okay," she sighed. "I'll play." She trudged onto the court.

The ball thumped on the concrete. Laughter rang through the yard.

"Point!"

"Foul!"

Reanna and Kody made a good team, but Jimmy Lee and Michael won the game. Vonnie came out frequently to cheer, and the players stopped only when it grew too dark to see.

Kody was having the time of his life. The basketball game brought back memories of Kyle and Christine. Every Saturday morning, when the weather was decent, Kody would play basketball with his brother, his sister, and his dad. Christine was the best player. She was quick and accurate with her shots. Kody loved to play on the same team as his sister. But he didn't get to play with her every Saturday. They always mixed the teams up but Christine and Kody were a formidable foe, when they were together. It was as close to victory on a basketball court as Kody could get, and he reveled in the friendly competition and desire to win. Sometimes he could almost hear a cheering crowd.

Reanna lightly punched Kody in the arm. "See," she said. "I did break a fingernail." She held out her hand for Kody to inspect.

"Maybe you should cut them all short," Kody suggested.

Reanna's eyes grew large. "It took me months to grow them out this long!"

"Well, now we know what we can get you for your birthday, Reenie," Jimmy Lee said. "Kody and I will pool our money and buy you a pair of fake nails."

Reanna pouted but there was a twinkle in her eyes.

They spilled into the kitchen, full of brag, teasing, and laughter. Vonnie sent them off to wash, then served up the crisp salads, soup, and homemade rolls. The talk around the table was lively. Kody went into detail about the upcoming Super Bowl and soon a spirited debate was taking shape about the outcome of the big game. They talked about their families and school and the wonderful season of summer. No religion. Kody forgot to worry. He could tell his parents liked the two girls very much. When he settled down on the couch with them, Vonnie brought buttery bowls of popcorn and said, "We're going to call Kyle and Christine. Any messages?"

"Tell them to bring reinforcements when they come home for spring break," quipped Kody. Everyone laughed. It felt like family.

After the last thrilling moments of *The Fugitive*, Michael and Vonnie reappeared to say good night to the two girls as Kody walked out to Reanna's car. "Thanks for coming," he yelled as they pulled away from the curb.

Kody couldn't believe his good fortune. It had been fun, not stressful at all. Everyone had had a good time. His parents had liked them. They'd liked his parents.

Kody paused in the driveway and looked skyward. Was there really a God? Had an all-powerful being blessed his house this afternoon? Things had certainly gone better than he had ever imagined. Kody let out a deep breath.

If there was a God and if He had granted Kody this favor, then what did He expect in return? What was the price? Suddenly the smugness left Kody, and he felt a new kind of responsibility, leaving him confused. Ever since he'd been a small child, his parents had taught him that nothing came free. Had he somehow placed himself under obligation to the Mormon god?

Kody wondered if gratitude would be enough. He lifted his eyes and whispered, "Thank you."

The stars winked back at him against the black expanse of the night sky.

Vonnie called, "Kody, dear. It's cold and you don't have your jacket."

"Come here for a minute, Mom."

Reluctantly, Vonnie walked out to stand by her son.

Kody pointed at the sky. "Isn't it beautiful?"

Vonnie followed his gaze. "Starry skies are always pretty."

"But it's more than a starry sky," Kody began. "It's a creation."

Vonnie put her arm around him. "Kody, you're freezing!" she said. "Come inside with me."

Kody silently obeyed, but his thoughts were far away, mingling with a Presence he felt sure had acknowledged him.

CHAPTER 8

Jimmy Lee scowled and picked up the prom photo sitting on her dresser. She was dressed in red satin and Mitch was wearing a black tux with a white shirt, red cummerbund, and bow tie. Then she smiled. They'd included Ruff on their date, and he wore a red bow tie for the occasion. He wasn't really a part of the activities. Mitch had kept him in the truck during dinner and the dance, but they saved some scraps for him and posed him next to them for their photo. He was irresistible, his eyes beaming, his tongue lolling in a lopsided doggy grin.

Sighing, she put the picture down. It had been fun. So many parts of her year with Mitch had been fun.

When Reanna had dropped her off, she had asked, "Do you want me to stay?" Jimmy Lee, though grateful, had refused. Mitch was gone. She needed to deal with it. For the past week she had grimly forced herself into her homework and chores, telephoning friends if there was even a spare moment; but every time she was alone it was always the same. Mitch would steamroll his way into her thoughts, flattening every defense. When would this obsessive phase end? And did she want it to end?

The questions pained her. Even though she knew Mitch was gone, sometimes thinking of him and the fun things they enjoyed together would soothe the ache. But there was always a moment when she crashed, realizing that, no matter how soothing the memories were, that's all they would ever be— memories. Never again would she go cross-country skiing with

Mitch and Ruff. She would not share in his triumphs during basketball season. She loved basketball, but now she stayed away from the games. She simply didn't dare attend. Just the thought of seeing Mitch in action was enough to keep her away. Knowing Brenda Timmins would be seated in her old place, right behind the players—no, she could never bear to attend.

Pulling on her winter coat, Jimmy Lee walked through the house to the patio door. When her mother gave her a look of concern, she said, "I just want a little night air."

Neither of her parents said anything about her situation, but she knew they were worried. She appreciated their concern but there wasn't anything they could do to help.

Jimmy Lee sat down on the bench under a maple tree and looked through the bare branches into the night sky. Before the breakup, she had never minded the cold. She was warm with Mitch. Usually after a date he would pull her close to him and they would lean against his truck and talk.

But not every evening was so nice. She remembered a night in early December when he had pulled over into a dead-end road. Every nerve in Jimmy Lee's body had tingled, and she feebly tried to rehearse in her head all of her reasons for denying Mitch the very thing she knew he would be asking for again.

Moving closer, he began to nuzzle her neck. Jimmy Lee loved his warmth and felt herself relaxing. Almost against her will, she pulled away. "No, Mitch," she said softly.

"Why not?" he asked.

"We've talked about this before," she said. "You know I can't do this."

He kissed her again. "You know you want to, Jimmy Lee," he said seductively in her ear.

She wished he didn't know how strong her feelings were.

Mitch whispered, "I've been planning this for a long time."

Suddenly she stiffened and pulled away sharply. "Mitch, I can't do this," she insisted.

Mitch smiled slowly. "Sure you can."

A thought crept into Jimmy Lee's mind. "Have you done this sort of thing before?"

Mitch hesitated, and Jimmy Lee knew the answer. "You don't have to tell me," she said. "I think I know."

"It was a long time ago, Jimmy Lee. Before I moved here. I didn't even know you then."

A deep and abiding sadness filled Jimmy Lee. "I can't do this, Mitch," she said. "It wouldn't be right."

"We love each other, don't we? What else matters?" His tone showed his frustration.

"Did you love the other girl? Will you love those who come after me?" she asked. "There's more at stake here, Mitch, than you understand." Then she added softly, "Even more than I understand."

"If you're worried about AIDS—"

"It's not that," she said. Suddenly she became overwhelmingly tired. How many times had she tried to explain this to Mitch? "Will you take me home, please?"

Mitch slid behind the wheel. The drive home was silent, and Mitch didn't walk her to the door.

When Jimmy Lee walked into her home and saw her family sitting around the dining room table eating ice cream, she knew she had done the right thing. The very idea of how close she had come to considering Mitch's proposal made her face color with shame. She could only imagine how it would feel to be unclean before her family and before the Lord.

But later, alone in her bedroom, Jimmy Lee cried. Things between her and Mitch would never be the same, and her heart ached for the more carefree days they had shared. A new kind of desperation seeped into her thoughts. She prayed urgently that somehow she and Mitch would be able to resolve this conflict without dooming their love. She knew now that Mitch really made up his mind that night.

A cold wind rattled the branches. Jimmy Lee pulled her coat tighter around her and shivered. Why hadn't she taken seriously her parents' cautions about dating a nonmember? If she had listened, she would have been able to avoid this pain. But then she wouldn't have known Mitch. Wasn't it better to have loved, despite the pain? And was it really hopeless? Hesitantly, she explored her deepest wish. Would Mitch come back to her? She knew she should not want him back. She should be glad he was gone, but oh how she missed him! Maybe after he'd had his fill of Brenda Timmins he might realize her own worth. Jimmy Lee closed her eyes against the cold air and clung to the thought of Mitch returning. It was her only hope.

The sound of the glass door sliding aside made her tense. Her father joined her on the bench. He was wearing his ski jacket but he shivered elaborately. "It's cold out here."

Jimmy Lee nodded.

"How did your afternoon with Kody and Reanna go?"

Jimmy Lee smiled. "It was fun. Kody's folks are nice, and Reenie even played some basketball."

They both laughed. Wes continued, "The two of you are kind of opposites but you've been friends for a long time. Where does Kody fit in all of this?"

"I'm not sure exactly but it's not romantic. He's steady and easy to be with. I appreciate that. He sees right through Mitch and Brenda. Everybody else at school has just accepted them as a couple. It's as if Mitch and I never existed."

"And Kody is different?"

"It's not like *he* talks about Mitch, but if *I* needed to, I know he'd listen. It's kind of nice to know a boy and be friends without all the romantic strings." She sighed. "I'm not anxious for another romance. Not for a long time."

Wes gave his daughter a hug. "I love you, Jimmy Lee, and I worry about you. I know how hard school is when things aren't going right."

Jimmy Lee hugged her father back. "Thanks, Dad. I love you too, but don't worry."

"Don't stay out too much longer," Wes said. "It's cold and you don't need frostbite."

Jimmy Lee smiled. "Okay, Dad."

Wes Donovan walked back inside and Jimmy Lee turned back to the cold, hushed yard. It was waiting for spring to bring it out of its deep sleep. Jimmy Lee understood the maples and dry grass. She, too, felt as if she were waiting.

CHAPTER 9

Sitting in the back of Sunday School class, Jimmy Lee only partially listened to the lesson.

"What did you do last night when you got home?" Reanna whispered.

Jimmy Lee shrugged. "Not much," she whispered back. "What about you?"

"Logan Goodwin called and asked if I wanted to catch the second half of the basketball game, but I said no."

"Not on my account, I hope," Jimmy Lee replied.

But before Reanna could continue their conversation, Sister Trenton asked the girls to either share their conversation with the whole class or listen to the lesson. They smiled apologetically and settled down until class was over.

On their way to Young Women, Jimmy Lee persisted. "I really hope you didn't stay home because of me, Reenie."

"Of course I stayed home because of you," snapped Reanna. "What makes you think I want to see Mitch strutting his stuff on the basketball court any more than you do? Especially when I lined you up."

"You didn't know how things would turn out," Jimmy Lee reasoned.

"You're certainly right about that. I thought you'd start dating a lot of different guys after that first date. Besides, Mitch was such a sweetheart. I had no idea he could be such a scum."

"Did you know that the only reason he went out with me that night was because of you?" Jimmy Lee asked.

"No way!" retorted Reanna. "That's not true at all. He said he liked your style and wanted to get to know you better."

"Well, not like he wanted to get to know *you*," Jimmy Lee said. "He told me after we'd been dating for a while. When you asked if he wanted to double, he thought it would be a good way to get to know you. I may have style, Reenie, but you're a knockout."

Reanna shook her head, still refusing to believe it. "Well, his attraction for me was short-lived. After that night he wouldn't let you out of his sight."

Jimmy Lee laughed. "He said you were too big a flirt."

Jimmy Lee smiled as they signed the roll, the memory bittersweet. Reanna had been dating Ken Mackley then. All three picked her up the Saturday after her sixteenth birthday. Mitch was attentive, courteous, responsive, even gallant. They had dinner at the Cloak Room, one of the finer restaurants in town, then attended a school play. Mitch was driving, so he dropped off Ken and Reanna at their respective homes, then took the long way home with Jimmy Lee. They enjoyed the early Christmas lights, and Jimmy Lee's pulse raced. She was sure she was the luckiest girl in the world. Here she was, sixteen years old, sitting with one of the best-looking and kindest boys in the whole school. Mitch was new in town and everyone was intrigued by this tall, handsome basketball player. By the time Mitch kissed her gently good night, Jimmy Lee knew she was in love.

The next morning Reanna, outraged, told her that Ken had come back after everyone was in bed and threw gravel at her window until she woke up. "He wanted to come in, the slug!" exclaimed Reanna. "He said he expected some payback for all the money he'd spent. I told him that if he didn't leave that minute, I'd call my father."

Ken did leave; but ever since then he had sneered and gibed at Reanna and her Mormon friends, mocking their "prissy" religious beliefs.

When Mitch had started spending a lot of time with Ken

after school had started this fall, Jimmy Lee voiced her concerns. Mitch had brushed them off. "He just tries to bully everybody," he said. "He's not really mean. He's more hot air than anything."

"Well, tell him to blow it in someone else's direction for a change, will you?" Jimmy Lee had asked. Mitch just laughed.

Jimmy Lee sighed. It would be so easy to blame Ken for the trouble between Mitch and her, but she had to be completely honest. Ken's presence only irritated the real issue dividing them. Sex.

Suddenly the bell rang. Jimmy Lee hadn't heard one word of the lesson. Well, at least she'd been quiet.

She stood up and looked at Reanna. "What are you thinking about?"

"That night we went out for your sixteenth birthday," she replied.

Jimmy Lee smiled. "Me too. That sure was fun, wasn't it?"

"Until Ken Mackley ruined it all. What a jerk! If I'd known what he was truly like, I wouldn't have gone out with him if he had been the last man on earth!"

"That's what playing the field does for you," Jimmy Lee teased.

Reanna shot her a look. "Well, there's no question about our beliefs now," she said. "Everyone in the whole school knows where we stand, thanks to Ken."

Jimmy Lee changed the subject. "Did you have a good time yesterday at Kody's?"

Reanna brightened. "You know, I did. Kody's a real sweetie and his folks seem nice too."

"Would you visit him again?"

"Absolutely. I'd love to."

Monday afternoon Jimmy Lee walked out into her backyard again. The maple branches were not full of stars, and the grass was shriveled, colorless. A cold mist shrouded the yard, graying and chilling the neighborhood.

She shivered. She wanted to retreat to the warmth and color of her room, but she had come to examine the flower beds edging the yard and patio. Even though it was cold and misty, the earth was not frozen, and it wasn't unusual for bulbs to bolt out of the soft soil in mid-January. She hoped they wouldn't come up so early, though. If there happened to be a hard frost the tender plants would wither under the cold and they wouldn't bloom. Zipping up her jacket, Jimmy Lee moved to the nearest bed and knelt on the grass. Clumps of leaves, left over from last autumn's raking, were deteriorating into brown patches here and there. But weeds were already growing, coarse, green, and vigorous. Thistle, rogue blackberry starts, and especially dandelions had spread everywhere. If she didn't hurry, they would quickly be established, fighting the bulbs and other spring flowers. A dandelion was even blooming, a radiant yellow flower in the middle of the brown and gray. She hesitated. It was almost irresistible. But she pressed her lips. If she let this one live, it would only go to seed and spread throughout the whole yard.

Dandelions were hard to get rid of because of their deep taproot, but Jimmy Lee, with gentle prodding and tugging, loosened this one, then yanked it up. Before it was dark she had finished weeding one of the biggest beds. Three to go.

She was so cold that the cozy warmth of the kitchen made her cheeks tingle. Then her mother exclaimed, "Jimmy Lee, you're a mess! What in the world have you been doing out there?"

Jimmy Lee looked down. Her best jeans were muddy and wet from the knee to the ankle; her jacket was smeared with mud where she had absently wiped her hands; and her cowboy boots were caked with debris. She looked up and grinned ruefully. "I've been weeding."

"And I've been mopping the kitchen floor," Beth said. "Please take your shoes off right where you are. Then go outside and scrape off the mud. Wait a minute." Beth returned with a clean pair of shoes.

Jimmy Lee removed one boot at a time, slipping on the clean shoes. "I'll clean up the floor," she said.

Beth had a moist paper towel ready. "I'll take care of it," she said.

Jimmy Lee went back to the patio, brushed away all the mud that would leave her pants and jacket, then cleaned her hands and set to work on her boots.

Her mother came out wrapped in a thick sweater and carrying her husband's heavy bathrobe. "Give me your pants and jacket and put this on," she demanded. "Now, hustle inside. I've got chocolate heating in the microwave."

Jimmy Lee obeyed, her teeth chattering. The microwave dinged as they stepped through the door. Beth hurried to the laundry room with the muddy clothes while Jimmy Lee wiped her boots clean with a damp paper towel. She put them on another towel close to the heat vent and took both steaming mugs from the microwave as her mother came back in.

Jimmy Lee pulled her chair over the floor vent, the hot air filling the tent made by her father's bathrobe. It felt delicious on her cold legs, and she savored the hot sweet milky chocolate's first swallow.

Beth sipped at her own mug. "The flower beds look much better," she said.

"I hope I can get to the other three before the bulbs start to come up."

"On cold days like this it feels like we have all the time in the world to plant our gardens, doesn't it?" Beth asked. "It's kind of like life."

"One of your parables, Mom?" Jimmy Lee grinned.

"Think about it," urged Beth. "For long stretches of our lives, we feel like we've got all the time in the world. Then one day we look around us. If we haven't been tending our gardens regularly, they're choked in weeds that block out the sunlight and take all the food and water."

Jimmy Lee thought about the dandelion. It had been a bright and yellow flower, but its only real promise was trouble.

Was Mitch a weed? He had crowded into her life. She'd never missed church but he'd robbed Reanna of her companionship. Robbed Jimmy Lee too, of a sixteenth year of openness, exploration, and growth in the gospel. She thought of flower beds; one prepared for blooming and the other next to it, drowning in weeds. She didn't have to guess which one would produce the spring bounty she was dreaming about.

Beth put her hand on her daughter's arm. "When we're free of Satan's entanglements, Jimmy Lee, we can grow beyond even our own ideas of potential."

Jimmy Lee nodded. She didn't feel like defending Mitch. Or herself. She drank her hot chocolate slowly.

Every inch ached for that hot shower, but on the way she paused and took one more look at the flower beds.

CHAPTER 10

Sitting with Jimmy Lee and Reanna during lunch, Kody was pleased to see that Jimmy Lee was regaining some spunk. She wasn't as quiet. She smiled more easily. Whenever she saw Mitch, either alone or with Brenda, she would look away. Sometimes tears would fill her eyes, but she wouldn't let it throw her.

Reanna was her usual bubbly self, and Kody couldn't help but feel drawn to her. Most of the boys at Pinecrest High felt the same way. Someone new was always dropping by their table for lunch. Watching Reanna flirt with the boys almost made Kody forget the question that had been tingling in his mind for the last two weeks: Is there a God? He needed to know.

After the morning spent at the stake center and the conversation with his folks, Kody was more confused than ever. For the past two weeks he'd been hoping for an opportunity to talk to the girls, but this was the first time they'd been alone. He blurted out, "There's something I'd like to ask the two of you. Is there a God?"

Jimmy Lee looked surprised but answered, "Yes, Kody, there is."

"How do you know?" he asked.

Both girls were silent. Then Jimmy Lee answered. "It's not something I. . . ." She looked at Reanna. "This is kind of hard to explain. I've never seen God or Jesus, but I know they exist. Sometimes when I'm living in a way that pleases my Heavenly Father I can feel Him close to me."

Kody looked at Reanna. "What about you? Do you believe in God?"

"Yes."

"But how? How can you believe in something you haven't seen for yourself?" Kody asked.

"There really isn't any easy way to explain it," she said. "It's a feeling. Something that comes from inside." Reanna put her hand to her heart.

Jimmy Lee said, "It's a matter of faith, Kody. I have faith that God exists. It's one of those times when I trust my feelings."

"Yeah. That's it," Reanna said. "Faith."

"What's faith?"

"It's a belief in something that can't be seen," Jimmy Lee explained.

"Do you believe in God?" Reanna asked.

Kody looked at the pretty blonde and shook his head. "I don't know what to believe," he answered honestly. Then he asked, "How did you get this faith?"

Jimmy Lee said, "I think every person has the ability to recognize our Heavenly Father."

"How?" Kody asked.

Reanna continued. "Everybody is born with the light of Christ that helps us recognize and distinguish the good from the bad."

"Like a conscience?" Kody asked.

"Exactly," Jimmy Lee said. Then she became excited. "The light of Christ is like that but it's a spiritual thing."

"Do I have this light of Christ?" Kody asked.

"Sure you do," Reanna said. "Have you ever done anything wrong and deep inside you know it's wrong? That's your conscience—the light of Christ helping you tell the difference between right and wrong."

"It can work the other way too," Jimmy Lee added. "Whenever you do something right, your conscience, or that special light, will encourage you. You'll feel warm inside and lighter. You know you're doing a good thing."

Kody thought about the Saturday night when he had looked into the starry sky with a heart full of gratitude. The feelings Jimmy Lee was describing sounded oddly familiar. He *had* felt warm inside. Could it be because of the light of Christ? "Can somebody lose this special light?" he asked.

Reanna furrowed her brow. "I don't know for sure, but I think some folks must lose it. How else could they continue to do bad things if they listened to their conscience? After a while it must be easier to rationalize the things we do. I think everybody's that way. Keeping the light takes a little work, I guess."

"If someone has lost it, they can get it back by repenting," Jimmy Lee said. "By turning away from the darkness and concentrating on light—on doing good things."

"Does everybody really have this light? Do I?" Kody wondered.

Jimmy Lee looked at him intensely. "Heavenly Father doesn't play favorites," she said. "It's available to everyone. Just like the sunshine. What do you feel inside, Kody? You may not feel you have faith, but do you have even a bit of a pulling toward it? A curiosity to understand it? A desire to believe in God?"

Kody hesitated. "I think I might," he said cautiously.

Jimmy Lee felt a powerful surge of mingled excitement and regret. How many times had she tried to have this conversation with Mitch? Twice? Three times? He'd always turned the topic aside with a deft and easy compliment. She had felt awkward and juvenile in persisting, so soon gave up trying. But what had she done to *her* light? She hadn't turned from the light. It had just become—well, dimmer. Diminished. It was a disturbing thought.

Reanna was excitedly rushing on. "That's where faith begins. With a desire to believe. Then you need to make room for it to grow. Do your folks believe in God?"

"Not in so many words. Mom said she believes in a supreme being, but I'm not too sure about Dad. He says Christianity is just a big business."

Jimmy Lee's eyebrows shot up.

"You know," Kody explained. "Like the guys on TV who are always asking you to donate money."

Jimmy Lee nodded.

The bell rang.

"Would you like to talk some more about God?" Reanna asked.

Kody hesitated. "I guess so. No. I *do.*"

CHAPTER 11

Sitting in church between Jimmy Lee and Reanna, Kody felt uneasy at the newness of the experience but also quite proud. He was surrounded by beauty. Both girls looked exceptionally pretty, but Reanna really sparkled in a dress of emerald green.

On Wednesday, Jimmy Lee had asked Kody if he wanted to attend church and Kody had accepted the invitation, deciding that if he truly was going to find out about God he would have to jump in with both feet. His parents were dubious at first, but Kody explained the conversation in detail. He made sure they understood why he was pursuing the matter and that the girls weren't pushing him. They gave their permission and said he could take the car, but their expressions were concerned.

After his decision was made, the week seemed to drag by, creating an edge of anxiety and excitement in Kody. What would church be like? What would be expected of him? The girls had said there would be singing and talks but that nobody would ask him to do anything. Now here he sat, between his two friends. Both girls made him feel welcome and introduced him to their families. Jimmy Lee's dad looked different in a white shirt, tie, and suit. Both Reanna's parents and Jimmy Lee's folks seemed genuinely happy to have him attend. He wished his parents were here. He thought they would like Wes and Beth Donovan and the Lewises, Chet and Anna.

Kody had liked the singing. His ability to read music let him join in with confidence. He hadn't been sure what to do about the trays of bread and water that were passed around after separate prayers; but Jimmy Lee had quietly whispered, "Just pass it on to me." The boys passing the bread and water row by row were younger than he was. Joseph and Scott had taken turns praying.

Kody had expected a sermon by a clergyman, but a member of the congregation was speaking—Sister Thornton, the bishop's wife. She was talking about the importance of serving one another. The message held his attention most of the time.

Three hours later Kody's stomach was growling and his head was spinning. He could hardly remember any of the words spoken in Sunday School or the meeting everyone called Priesthood. Everyone was friendly, though.

"Well, what did you think?" Reanna asked as they walked out to the parking lot.

Kody shook his head. "How do you keep it all straight?" he asked. "Aren't the two of you tired?"

Jimmy Lee shook her head. "No, not really, but it does take some time to get used to it. Three hours is a long time, so don't expect it to be a breeze the first few times."

Kody was silent. He had been so worried about doing or saying something stupid that he hadn't really concentrated on the lessons. "Maybe it will be easier next week," he said.

Both girls smiled. "Give it some time," Reanna said with a pat on his shoulder. They waved as he drove out of the parking lot. Kody drove slowly, thinking. He was pleased that the focus of the meeting was service to one's fellow beings. But what would his parents think? Surely they would ask questions.

Kody walked into the living room. His folks were watching the Sunday afternoon basketball game.

Michael turned off the television when Kody walked into the family room. "How did it go?" he asked.

"It was very interesting," Kody said as he sat down. "But I must admit I'm tired."

"Three hours of meetings is a long time. What did they talk about?"

Kody explained about Sister Thornton's talk on service. He also talked about the Sunday School lesson that explained the parable of the Good Samaritan and a meeting called Priesthood where he'd been with other teenage boys. "Their lesson had been on something called the oath and covenant of the priesthood."

"Priesthood?" Michael said. "Oaths and covenants?" He looked alarmed.

Kody shook his head. "I'm not sure. I couldn't follow it. They didn't ask us to do anything weird. I didn't know if I could ask Reanna and Jimmy Lee since they're girls. I wasn't sure if they would know anything about it."

"So, it was just for the young men?"

"That was the class I was in. The girls were in a different class. But they have other classes for older men too. I kind of wished you and Mom were there. It would've been nice for you to meet the Donovans and Lewises."

"That'd be nice," Michael said. "But we don't have to go to church to meet them."

Kody nodded. He realized, even though he had not expected them to come, that he had really hoped they would. But meeting his friends and their families was really only part of the reason. All the information he was learning was so new and different. He found himself wishing he could talk it over with his parents.

"We sure have missed your oboe practices the last couple of days," Vonnie said.

"Yeah. I need to practice, I guess. Mr. Svenson is having me work on music interpretation." Kody thought about Mr. Svenson's words about playing music instead of just notes. If he was going to look at the music with a clear mind, he needed some lunch. "Before I practice, I need to eat something. I'm starved."

"There's a ham sandwich in the fridge."

After lunch, Kody had to fight off the desire to take a nap, something he hadn't done since he was four. Instead he pulled out his oboe case and began to assemble his instrument. The gleaming black wood and polished silver keys were comfortingly familiar.

He tried to shut out the sports heroes that looked down on him with smug and successful smiles. But as he moved his fingers through his arpeggios and scales the posters seemed to leap to life, making it difficult to concentrate. He could picture Michael Jordan sailing through the air for a slam dunk but he couldn't picture moving notes into phrases or swelling with love or passion.

Closing his eyes, Kody tried to remember what Mr. Svenson had asked him to work on during his last lesson. He had asked Kody to be patient and continue to think of his new friends when he played a piece.

With his eyes still closed, Kody moved his fingers over the keys. He played a piece by the composer Vivaldi. He knew the music from memory. Still the feelings would not come. They were buried under confusion, fatigue, and frustration.

Blowing hard into his oboe, he made a high-pitched squeaking sound before he began putting his instrument away. Mr. Svenson was asking for too much. No one could think of more than one thing at a time.

As he put his oboe in its velvet-lined case, Kody could hear the basketball game on the television. Involuntarily his eyes were drawn to the picture of Michael Jordan. Chicago was playing today. From the roar of the crowd and his father's excited outbursts Kody could tell it was a good game.

Without a backward glance Kody joined his father. "Who's winning?" he asked.

"Chicago."

Kody settled down into the couch and cradled the fresh bowl of popcorn his mother handed him.

"Hey, don't forget to share," Michael said as he reached over and grabbed a handful of popcorn.

Kody grinned and placed the bowl on the coffee table, where everyone could reach. Soon he forgot all about the popcorn and his oboe as he concentrated on the game.

Still in her Sunday clothes, Jimmy Lee wandered restlessly around her room. She studied the walls. Pictures of her and Mitch hung in frames on her wall, along with the collage of snapshots on her bulletin board. Hesitantly she lifted one of the framed photos, but she quickly returned it to the wall, checking to make sure it was straight.

"I should hate him," she mumbled to herself, wishing she could. It would make things so much easier. But even when she sat down and tried to muster up ill will, nothing happened—just the old familiar ache came back.

One thing made her glad. People at school had stopped offering their condolences. But even people who didn't like Brenda had begun including her. Given Mitch's success on the basketball court, everyone wanted to be a part of a winning season.

Jimmy Lee covered her face with her hands. "I've got to get out of this room," she muttered. Flinging the door open she hurried to the kitchen, where her mother was preparing dinner.

"Can I help?" she asked.

"Sure, honey," Beth Donovan said. "I was just about to make some pudding for dessert."

Jimmy Lee smiled and pulled the milk out of the refrigerator. "I'll do it," she said.

CHAPTER 12

The following Friday, Jimmy Lee settled into her seat for study hall.

Reanna sat down in front of her and turned around. "What do you say we go to the game tonight, Jimmy Lee?" She looked at her questioningly. "It's been four weeks and the team is doing so well."

"I don't know," Jimmy Lee said with trepidation. "I'm not sure I'm ready for that."

"C'mon, Jimmy Lee. It'll be fun. I'll be with you and Kody will come too. Joseph and Scott asked about you this morning. They miss your expert commentary on the game."

Jimmy Lee loved basketball—but seeing Brenda? Seeing Mitch?

Reanna seemed to read her mind. "You can't always hide out, Jimmy Lee, because you're afraid of who you'll see," she said softly.

"Okay, I'll go, but I want to sit somewhere else—not right in front, like we used to."

"Sure," Reanna promised.

Jimmy Lee was nervous as Reanna pulled into a parking place.

"Don't worry," Reanna said briskly, grabbing her hands. "It'll all be fine. You have just as much right to be here as anyone."

As the girls moved through the crowded gymnasium,

Jimmy Lee began to relax. Everywhere she turned people were smiling and waving, obviously glad to see her. Rick Morris gave her an ear-to-ear grin and bounded up the bleachers to sit by them. They waved at Kody until he finally located them. Joseph and Scott climbed down from the top row. They made a solid group halfway up the bleachers and mid-court.

"Perfect!" Jimmy Lee said. She was surprised at how good it felt to be there. She had expected to feel heart-wrenching pain in watching Mitch's smoothly muscled body, but instead she found herself caught up in the tension of the game. The point spread between the two teams was tight. During half-time, friends crowded around and the discussion of strategy for the second half was a lively squabble. Then the team came out of the locker room and Jimmy Lee saw a harsh blonde head and craned her neck to see better. Brenda walked straight up to Mitch, who was shooting baskets from the side-line. Her lips were moving fast and her face was angry.

Jimmy Lee stared curiously. "What do you think is going on?" she asked Reanna.

Reanna shrugged. "I don't know, but the way the rumor mill works around here I bet we'll have a good idea before the game is over."

Brenda's face continued to deepen in color, an ugly scowl settling in. Jimmy Lee glanced down at Mitch, who was balancing the basketball on one hip. She saw the other boys on the team beginning to drift toward their star player. They were obviously embarrassed by the scene.

The coach walked over and said something to Brenda. She walked away. Jimmy Lee saw defeat in her slumped shoulders.

Warm-ups continued for a few more minutes, then the whistle blew for the tip-off. Jimmy Lee could not concentrate on the game. It didn't matter that the score seesawed or that her school team was fighting for home court advantage in the state tournament. Her eyes were glued on Mitch. A nameless hope swelled inside, as did a confusion of other emotions. Most of all, she was curious. What was Brenda so upset about?

Why was Mitch so adamant? Was this the end of their relationship? Jimmy Lee forced herself to watch the game and join in the cheers. The last thing she wanted was for Mitch to find out that she was frantic about his argument with Brenda. She didn't dare even look at Reanna.

During the fourth quarter Reanna poked at Jimmy Lee's ribs. Brenda rose from her seat, the seat Jimmy Lee had always sat in, wiping her eyes ostentatiously.

"I didn't realize she was so dramatic," Reanna whispered. "If she's looking for sympathy, it's the wrong approach. No one is going to appreciate her if she makes Mitch lose his focus."

Jimmy Lee nodded, thoughts racing through her mind. She looked down at the seat Brenda had just vacated. An overwhelming desire filled Jimmy Lee. What if she just walked down there in front of the whole student body and reclaimed that seat? Mitch would surely take her back if he looked up and saw this visible sign of support after Brenda had been so ugly.

Then Jimmy Lee felt a warm hand on hers. It was Kody. "Don't do it," he said. "Don't do it, Jimmy Lee."

Tears flooded her eyes and she gripped Kody's hand. He was right, of course. She tried to brush the tears from her eyes, but they kept coming. Kody discreetly produced a handkerchief. Jimmy Lee gratefully bowed her head and wiped her eyes, hoping no one had seen.

Just then Lanie Steward bounced up the aisle. "You'll never guess what happened," she said. "Brenda asked Mitch to go to her folks' cabin for the weekend. Her whole family is going to be there, and her parents told her she could invite Mitch." Her voice dropped a notch. "Only, he won't go." Lanie looked at Jimmy Lee. "You know how Mitch is about drugs and alcohol."

Jimmy Lee nodded and explained to Kody. "He absolutely refuses to drink or take any kind of drugs because he takes his training really seriously. He's hoping to get into UCLA on a scholarship."

Lanie nodded and added, eyes wide, "Well, Brenda's parents are super heavy drinkers and they even do some drugs."

Her tone became conspiratorial. "I mean, we've all heard about Brenda's parties when her folks are supposed to be chaperoning. Anyway, Mitch told Brenda he wouldn't go."

"Is that what all the fuss was about?" Reanna asked.

Lanie nodded. "Brenda wanted Mitch to meet her family. She's got relatives coming from out of state. This is supposed to be a big family reunion."

Jimmy Lee swallowed but didn't trust herself to say anything.

Lanie looked up at the scoreboard. "Looks like we'll win this one," she said. "The Eagleridge team sure gives us a run for our money. Well, I should get back down there. Chris will be looking for me." She hurried down to her seat. Jimmy Lee had once been a part of "girlfriend group," the girls who sat right behind the team's bench and cheered their boys on until they were hoarse.

The buzzer sounded. The crowd roared. Jimmy Lee rose, cheering and clapping mechanically. She could see Mitch surrounded by his delirious teammates. He had made the winning point.

Jimmy Lee sighed, feeling depressed. Coming had probably been a bad idea.

"Hey, Jimmy Lee," said Joseph. "Let's go to the Scone Haus."

Jimmy Lee shook her head. "Um, thanks, but I don't think so."

"Everyone will be there," Joseph insisted.

"That's the point," snapped Reanna. "I'll drop you off first and then I'll go on over."

"I'll take Jimmy Lee home," Kody offered as they began to file out of the gymnasium.

Reanna looked at Jimmy Lee, who answered, "That would be great, Kody, if you don't mind."

"Not at all," Kody replied.

Reanna hugged Jimmy Lee. "I think you're brave," she whispered. "And I'm glad you came."

Kody and Jimmy Lee threaded their way through the

maze of cars and kids without speaking. Jimmy Lee kept her head down against the glare of lights in the parking lot, but she still couldn't shut out the jumble of laughter and excited voices celebrating the victory. She felt like an outsider—remote from the happy moment. Her heart wasn't in the win. All she could think about were the many victories she had shared with Mitch.

Then, as if her very thoughts conjured up his image, she heard Mitch's voice. "Jimmy Lee?"

Jimmy Lee stopped short and looked up. Mitch stood directly in front of her. Kody stood silently at her shoulder. "Mitch?" she whispered.

Mitch smiled, and Jimmy Lee felt as if her heart would unravel in her chest. Maybe he had broken up with Brenda. Her hopes soared high into the night sky.

"What did you think of the game?" he asked.

"You were wonderful, Mitch," Jimmy Lee gushed. Then she was immediately sorry she had lost her composure. "I mean, it's great that the team will have home court advantage now," she retreated.

Mitch's smile broadened as he nodded. "I think we've got a good chance at the state championship."

Jimmy Lee swallowed hard, her throat constricting her voice. All she could do was nod.

Mitch shoved his hands into his pockets. "Well, it's good to see you, Jimmy Lee," he said before moving off.

Jimmy Lee felt frantic. Inside, she was screaming for him to turn around and say he wanted her back. She forced herself to stand and watch him, afraid to blink for fear of losing him in the mass of kids. Then he disappeared. Mechanically, at the touch of Kody's hand on her elbow, she stepped forward, but tears were blurring her vision. As she climbed into Kody's car she no longer could control her anguish. Doubling over in the passenger seat, she buried her face in her hands and sobbed.

After a long minute Kody reached over and placed his hand on her shoulder. "That was hard, wasn't it?" Kody said.

"I shouldn't have come," she sobbed. "Did you hear the way I reacted when I saw him? I turned into a complete idiot. I gushed all over him! I'm so embarrassed."

"So what if you gushed all over him? People gush over Mitch all the time. He didn't even notice. Besides, after dating you for a whole year I think he knows you're not a gusher." He handed her his handkerchief again.

Jimmy Lee looked up and blinked. "You think so?"

"Of course. Besides, you need to quit concentrating on what *he* thinks and start concentrating on what *you* think."

Jimmy Lee straightened up and blew her nose. "You're right, Kody," she said. She wiped the tears. "There's something else. I want to thank you for your common sense during the game. What I was thinking of doing would've been really stupid and humiliating."

"I could see it in your eyes," he said. Then he smiled. "Hey, what are friends for, right?"

Jimmy Lee returned his smile. "This isn't the first time you've come between me and my own stupidity," she said.

Kody squeezed Jimmy Lee's hand. She relaxed against the headrest. "I hope he's sorry someday," she said.

"He will be," Kody replied with assurance. "I can guarantee it. Girls like you don't come along very often, Jimmy Lee. Mitch is the one who's stupid for not being able to see that. Someday he'll figure it out." He started the engine.

Jimmy Lee turned toward the window and watched the cars go by. She thought about the many prayers she had offered up, asking, sometimes begging, that the pain be taken away or that Mitch would magically appear on her doorstep. Neither one of those things had happened. Instead, she was being blessed with good friends like Reanna, who forced her to come out of her shell, and like Kody, whose gentle good sense always helped her keep her equilibrium.

Closing her eyes, Jimmy Lee silently acknowledged her blessings to her Heavenly Father. In spite of the hurt, He truly was looking after her.

As Kody pulled up in front of the house, Jimmy Lee sat up. "Why don't you come in for a minute?" she asked.

"Okay, thanks," he responded.

He was pleased at how warmly Jimmy Lee's parents greeted him. Wes immediately began fixing hot chocolate all around, and Allison came out of her bedroom and cut a panful of brownies as Jimmy Lee and Kody reported on the game.

"Where's Reanna?" Beth asked.

"She decided to go to the Scone Haus, and Kody offered to bring me home," Jimmy Lee said.

"Jimmy Lee, are you all right? You look tired," Wes said. "Hand me the marshmallows, will you?"

Jimmy Lee opened the drawer and found the marshmallows next to the chocolate chips. "We ran into Mitch on the way to the car," she explained. "It took a lot out of me."

"Wow!" exclaimed Allison. "What did he say? What did *you* say?"

"I was stupid," Jimmy Lee said flatly as she moved to the couch. She retold her story, adding Kody's words of advice.

Beth nodded approvingly, picking up crumbs from her brownie. "Kody's right, honey. You need to quit focusing your attention on Mitch and start thinking about things you'd like to be doing."

Jimmy Lee nodded, trying to think of things she enjoyed. During the last year all her free time had been spent with Mitch. What could she do that didn't include him? Then she remembered something and she sat up straight. "The flower beds! I like taking care of the flowers. Mitch never helped me because he didn't like it. Said he got too muddy."

Kody smiled. "See, I knew you could think of something."

Wes added, "And if you gave it some more thought, I bet you could come up with a whole list of things you like to do."

"You could take me shopping," Allison said hopefully.

Jimmy Lee pretended to scowl. "This is supposed to be fun!" Then she became thoughtful. "I bet you're right, Dad," she said quietly. "I'm sure I can think of a lot of fun things. But

I sure have missed the flower beds. Last spring I didn't spend any time with the flowers."

"Well, spring is just around the corner, so you can make up for lost time," Beth said.

Kody drained the last of his hot chocolate. He stood up. "Great brownies, Mrs. Donovan. Thanks for cutting me the biggest piece, Allison."

Everyone laughed.

Jimmy Lee walked out to Kody's car with him. "Thanks for bringing me home," she said. "And thanks for being such a good friend."

Kody smiled, warmed by the hot chocolate and the bond that was beginning to form between him and Jimmy Lee.

Jimmy Lee looked around her room. Every wall hung with memories of Mitch. Slowly she walked to the collage on her bulletin board and took it down. With gentle fingers she touched each photograph as she remembered the events that had shaped their relationship: the picture of Mitch, with tousled hair, standing in the snow, his skis and Ruff at his side. Last year's championship game where he held the trophy high, his hair damp with sweat. She peeled them away from the backing and put them in a manila envelope. She saved out one photo. A snapshot of her and Ruff. The dog was panting and covered with snow after a frolic in the mountains. He stood beside her, tongue lolling, looking happily at the camera.

Gazing at the picture longingly, she propped it against the prom picture sitting on her dresser before placing the manila envelope in the back of her closet. When she returned to her room she stared thoughtfully at the blank bulletin board and was surprised to find she liked the empty space. Kody was right. It was time for her to start thinking of things she enjoyed doing that didn't include Mitch. Maybe she could go cross-country skiing with someone else. Someone like Kody, a good friend. Closing her eyes, Jimmy Lee let out a long sigh. Maybe she was beginning to take back the pieces of the life she had so freely given to Mitch.

Kody's parents were watching the eleven o'clock news. "Who won?" Michael asked. "Did you have a good time?"

Kody nodded. "Yeah. Except Jimmy Lee ran into her old boyfriend in the parking lot and cried her eyes out once we got into the car. Poor girl. She really felt horrible, but I took her home and we talked for a bit. I think she feels better."

Vonnie smiled. "She's lucky to have you for a friend."

"Actually, I'm the one who feels lucky. Both her and Reanna are great to be around."

Michael flipped to a new station. Kody sat down on the couch with a yawn. Half of his attention was on the evening he had just spent with Reanna, Jimmy Lee, and the basketball game. He was glad he had been there when Jimmy Lee had needed a friend. It felt good to do something for someone else. He remembered the talk Sister Thornton had given in church the week before. Was this what she meant by serving others?

Kody looked at his parents, who were watching the news with bored expressions. Church was the day after tomorrow. He'd procrastinated all week. Now he needed to tell them that he wanted to attend again.

"Mom, Dad?" he tried to sound casual. "Would it be okay with you if I attend church again on Sunday?"

Vonnie and Michael looked at each other briefly, then Michael spoke. "Kody, your mother and I have talked about this. We never want to hold you back from exploring these issues that seem so important to you, but. . . ."

Vonnie chimed in. "But we just don't understand this new fascination with religion. Isn't one Sunday enough? I know Jimmy Lee and Reanna are good girls, but you've only invited them to the house once. Is what they have to offer so much more appealing than what you have at home?"

"Oh, Mom, it's nothing like that—"

"Maybe you just really miss your brother and sister."

Kody paused. He hadn't thought of that. Maybe he found Jimmy Lee and Reanna so attractive because he missed his Kyle and Christine. No, he really didn't think so. He did miss them, but Kyle had been gone for two years and Christine for one. His feelings for Reanna and Jimmy Lee didn't change his missing his brother and sister. "I don't think that's it, Mom," he explained. "You see, I've never really had any friends of my own before this. Kyle and Christine and their friends always accepted me and it was fine, but for the first time I've made friends on my own."

"Does that mean you'll turn your back on your family for these new friends?" Michael asked. His voice was cool.

"No. That's not it at all! Listen, why don't you come to church with me on Sunday? Then you can meet the Lewises and Donovans for yourself, and you'll understand why I find their church so interesting."

Vonnie shook her head. "Kody, you know how important Sunday is to us. It's the only day of the week your father and I know we're going to be home together. I don't want to spend it with a bunch of people I don't know."

"So, are you telling me I can't go?"

Vonnie glanced away from his face, sighed, and shook her head once again. "No. I don't have the heart to withhold permission. I guess I just wish you would *choose* to spend the day here with us."

Kody looked down. He hated the thought of disappointing his parents. But maybe they were disappointing him. Why couldn't they go to church just one Sunday so they could realize why this was so important? "Mom, I really need to see this through and understand it."

For a brief moment, the only noise in the room came from the television weatherman. Then Vonnie slowly nodded. "We won't hold you back, Kody, but we feel we owe it to you to let you know how we feel and this isn't our first choice for you."

"I understand," Kody said. Slowly, he walked down the hall to his bedroom.

CHAPTER 13

On Saturday morning Beth woke Jimmy Lee early and told her to hurry and dress. Bewildered, Jimmy Lee obeyed. Thirty minutes later she sat at the breakfast table and peppered her mother with questions, but Beth would only smile. "It's a surprise," she said.

After breakfast Beth hurried Jimmy Lee to the car. They drove out of town to the animal shelter, and Beth announced, "We want you to choose a puppy."

Jimmy Lee's eyes lit up and she gasped in delight.

Beth continued. "I've talked with your father and with Allison, and we agreed that our family needs a dog. However, you'll be responsible for it. If it needs to go to the vet, you'll take it. When it's time for obedience school, you'll see to it. You'll feed, bathe, walk, and otherwise care for this new member of our family. And you'll clean up after it, too. The back yard is already fenced, so there should be plenty of room."

Jimmy Lee felt as if her fondest wish was being granted. But her choice would be difficult. At the animal center so many dogs looked at her with confused and sad eyes, begging to be taken home. Some barked and yapped excitedly at every newcomer that walked by, while others looked anxious and miserable. Tears choked in her throat and she took her mother's hand. "They all need to be cared for," she said.

"I know, honey, and I wish I could tell you that all of them will find a good home. Some of them won't be so lucky, but one will be very lucky—the one you choose to take home and love."

With a new resolution Jimmy Lee began to look inside each kennel again. There were dogs of all ages and mixed breeds, and she said a silent prayer to help her make the best choice for her and her family. Several times she walked up and down the cement hallways, but she returned again and again to one puppy, apparently the last of her litter. She looked healthy—her coat was a beautiful golden color—but she seemed withdrawn. Sometimes she would tremble.

Jimmy Lee knelt down in front of the puppy's kennel and began talking to her gently. The puppy paid attention. Soon her tail was wagging, and she had inched forward until she could lick Jimmy Lee's fingers through the gate. Jimmy Lee could tell she would not be very big when full grown. When Beth came and stood beside her, Jimmy Lee rose. The puppy protested with a quiet whine.

"I want this one," Jimmy Lee said with conviction. "I want her."

"Okay," Beth said. "You wait here, and I'll go and talk with the folks at the front desk."

A few minutes later Beth returned with an animal control officer, who unlocked the door and scooped up the puppy.

"He thought it would be a good idea if we spent a few minutes with her before you made your final decision. They have a room where we can interact with her without any distractions."

Jimmy Lee nodded in agreement, but her decision was made. She looked at the officer. "How big do you think she'll get?"

"Well, I'd say she's a mix of several breeds but she probably will only weigh about ten to twenty pounds when fully grown. There were six in her litter. Her last brother just left an hour ago."

Jimmy Lee sat on the floor of the room and played with the puppy for several minutes. The dog was full of energy but couldn't always control her legs on the slippery floor. Jimmy Lee and Beth laughed as she lost her balance.

"Well, what do you say?" asked the officer when he returned.

"She's the one," Jimmy Lee replied. "When can I take her home?"

"You'll have to pay a licensing fee, sign a few papers saying you'll bring her back in six months to be spayed. Then she's yours."

Jimmy Lee grinned, feeling happier than she had in months. Hugging the ball of fur close, she smiled at her mother. "She's great, Mom. Thanks."

Beth smiled at her daughter. "I'm sure the two of you will be terrific friends."

Half an hour later they were settling in the car. The puppy was in the back seat in a cardboard kennel, communicating her displeasure with a volley of yaps.

"What are you going to name her?" Beth asked.

Jimmy Lee already knew—an outdoor name, a healthy, happy, name. "Clover," she exclaimed suddenly. "I'll call her Clover."

Later that day, when Clover was settled, Jimmy Lee called Reanna. Reanna squealed one question after another in an excited rush. "I'm so glad you have her." She sighed happily. "A puppy seems just right for you."

On Sunday morning Jimmy Lee followed her family out of the car and began walking to the chapel behind Allison and Beth. She had worried about leaving Clover, but Jimmy Lee had played with her until the puppy was exhausted. Clover had fallen asleep in her kennel before the family left for their meetings.

Jimmy Lee looked up at the blue sky. The night rain had freshened the air and the clouds had dispersed, leaving chilly sunshine streaming through the pine-scented air. Instead of walking toward the front door, she turned toward the flower beds, not caring that her best shoes and hose were getting wet.

Yes! Tiny green shoots were poking through the brown earth. The bulbs were coming alive. Excitement filled her and she bent down closer to the little miracles. She closed her eyes and felt tears. Mitch's excuse for not helping had rung hollow at the time. Now Jimmy Lee was glad. These flowers would be hers. Mitch had no part in their planting or in their growth, and when she looked at them it was a memory he could not touch.

Jimmy Lee heard the opening hymn and straightened quickly. She hurried inside and slipped into the pew beside Allison. Her father on the stand gave her a look and she mouthed an apology.

Glancing over the congregation, Jimmy Lee saw Kody sitting next to Reanna and her family. He really had come! She caught his eye and smiled. He nodded and grinned. Reanna winked at her.

Jimmy Lee's feet were freezing. She slipped off her wet shoes and slung her coat over her lap, wriggling her toes into a fold. She thought about the tender green shoots against the dark brown earth. "Consider the lilies of the field," she thought. A peace settled over Jimmy Lee. Yes. Soon her favorite flowers would be in bloom.

After the sacrament, Kody tried to concentrate on the youth speaker. He was impressed with Kevin Sanders's ability to get up in front of a hundred people and give a talk, but Reanna's perfume distracted him. It came to him like warm ocean waves, pulling him under. Oh, how he wanted to be pulled under! How would it feel to hold Reanna close, to touch her hair? The idea gave him such an excited, warm feeling and he could feel the blood rush to his face. He glanced toward Jimmy Lee. She was looking at him. "She knows!" he thought to himself. He was humiliated. Church was no place for thoughts like this. Blushing, he stared fixedly at Kevin Sanders.

The choir sang. Then Sister Griffin spoke, a tall blonde woman wearing half-glasses. "My husband and I were bikers," she began. "We owned Harley Davidsons. We wore leather. We drank a lot and spent every last dime on drugs." Her voice dropped a notch. "We weren't even married then," she said. "Then one day these two young men came to our door. They were so squeaky clean and fresh that it almost hurt to look at them. Jeff and I hadn't seen young men without hair on their faces for years, and to be honest, we didn't know how to act."

A laugh rippled through the congregation and Kody looked around to see how others were responding. Wasn't this awfully personal stuff? But no one looked disapproving. All of the faces were open and inviting. Even Jimmy Lee had lost some of her pinched look and was watching Sister Griffin intently.

"They told us they were representatives from The Church of Jesus Christ of Latter-day Saints and asked to come in." She paused and continued more slowly. "I don't know what compelled me to open my door to those two young men on that Friday afternoon. All I know is that when they walked into our dumpy shack with drug paraphernalia lying around I immediately became ashamed. Here were two young men from a church and I didn't even have a clean place for them to sit." She shrugged. "But back then, I didn't even know if there was a God."

Kody leaned forward and looked hard at Sister Griffin as she went on.

"I hadn't been raised with any particular religion. My father was a microbiologist and my folks often told me that the human species evolved from lower forms of life eons ago and that when this life was over it was the end. I can remember as a child thinking how bleak it all seemed and wondering why there wasn't more to life. Then I met Jeff and we fell in love. In spite of all the things Jeff and I did that were wrong, we truly did love one another, and I can remember feeling very desperate sometimes. It broke my heart to think that, when one of us died, we'd never be able to know one another again. I never shared any of these feelings with him because I was afraid he would think I was nuts.

"But after the elders came and talked to us about God's plan for each of us, I felt hope for the first time. It was as if all the answers to my questions since childhood were inside these two young men and I wanted to extract every single one of them. So I began to ask them. Their answers seemed so simple and plain and it all made perfect sense. They stayed with us for two hours and I grilled them with questions, each time thinking they wouldn't be able to find the answer. But they always did and they always had scriptures to back them up. That's when we were introduced to the Book of Mormon."

Tears filled Sister Griffin's eyes, spilling onto her cheeks. "Now, here we are, five years later. We're sealed in the temple and we have two beautiful children. I know none of this would've been possible if it weren't for the gospel and what it has taught me about my elder brother, Jesus Christ. I truly believe the gospel not only saved my spiritual life but it saved my physical life as well, and for those two things I will be eternally grateful."

Kody marveled. This woman came from a more questioning background than he, yet she had been able to find out for herself whether there was a God.

He studied her closely. No trace of her past life showed itself. There was no hardness around her eyes and mouth. Her face was softer and more open than Brenda Timmins's. He also noticed how loving everyone in the congregation had been during the talk. A blanket of love encircled this woman. She must have felt incredibly safe to share such a story.

His mind was racing. What was this Book of Mormon? It must explain Mormonism. Where could he get one? And where were the two young men who had answered all her questions?

He jumped when Reanna handed him the hymn book and pointed to the first verse. "The Lord is my shepherd," he sang. "No want shall I know. . . ." He wished it could be true.

After the closing prayer Kody asked Reanna, "Do you have a Book of Mormon?"

Reanna nodded. "Sure. But you can have one of your own, if you like? They have a bunch of them in the bishop's office."

Jimmy Lee caught up with them as they left the chapel.

"Kody wants a Book of Mormon," Reanna explained.

"Great!" enthused Jimmy Lee. "You'll really like it."

"And what about those two young men Sister Griffin talked about?" Kody asked. "Where are they?"

"They were missionaries," Jimmy Lee said. "The Church asks every worthy young man to serve a two-year mission at the age of nineteen. So they're not around anymore."

"They're not?" Kody slumped, his disappointment obvious.

"It's okay," said Reanna. "There are more. They're all trained to do this type of work. They'd love to talk with you."

"When?"

"Well, I don't know." Reanna sounded surprised at the tension in his voice. "Let's go see if we can find the elders who are working in our ward boundaries."

They veered off toward the foyer, where Kody met two young men in dark suits. Sister Griffin was right. They did look squeaky clean. The two young men shook hands enthusiastically, introducing themselves as Elder Moore and Elder Young.

Jimmy Lee explained that Kody wanted to learn more about the gospel. Kody was pleased at how willingly they made an appointment with him. They agreed to come Wednesday evening at six-thirty to Jimmy Lee's house.

A few minutes later, Kody was holding a Book of Mormon. As he sat in Sunday School he traced the gold embossed letters with his fingers and wondered what mysteries this book would unfold. For the first time in his life Kody felt as if he had some direction. He truly was going to find out whether or not there was a God. He was embarking on a new and adventurous journey. He would be climbing mountains no one in his family had ever climbed, charting seas completely foreign to them, and discovering treasures that someday he hoped to share with them, regardless of what his findings were.

As he sat in Sunday School with a sturdy little book in his hands and an appointment with two missionaries willing to teach him about God, Kody knew that finally he was going to find what lived beyond the stars.

CHAPTER 14

Walking through the door of his home, Kody turned the front of the Book of Mormon against his leg. Getting a copy of the Book of Mormon and making an appointment with the missionaries had made perfect sense at the moment, but now Kody was going to have to explain his decisions. What would he say? How would his folks react?

The television was on, and Kody followed the sound to the family room. His folks were watching the Seattle Sonics play the Portland Trailblazers.

"Hi! I'm back," he called.

"Hi, Son," Vonnie said. "There's a sandwich in the fridge."

"Thanks, Mom." Kody went into the kitchen and grabbed the sandwich before hurrying to his room. He needed time to think. He changed into jeans and a sweatshirt, then flopped down on his bed and thumbed through the book. He couldn't wait to begin reading. He switched on his reading lamp, piled his pillows, and slowly ate his sandwich as he opened the dark blue book. Soon he was engrossed in the writings of Nephi. He barely heard the knock on the door.

"Kody?" his father called from the other side of the door.

Kody jumped and hurriedly put the book on the shelf. He wasn't ready to share it with his folks yet. "Come in," he said.

When his dad stepped into the room Kody knew something serious was on his mind. Thoughtfully, Michael closed the door and sat down on the edge of Kody's bed. "Kody, can I ask you something?"

"Sure," Kody said, trying to sound casual.

"Your mother and I have been wondering why you never bring your friends home. Whenever you study or spend any time with them, it's always at their homes or at school. We talked about this briefly the other day but we didn't get a real answer from you."

Kody thought for a moment. "Well, I don't know, Dad. It's just that their folks like them to be home, I guess. You remember how it was with Christine. You always preferred that she bring her friends home."

"Yes," Michael nodded slowly. "But we like all our kids to spend time at home and with you being the youngest—well we would just really like for you to invite them here more often."

Kody thought about the upcoming missionary meeting. It was scheduled to be held at Jimmy Lee's house and Kody really preferred it that way. He hoped his folks would come, but he didn't want it to be held at home. Too much tension.

Michael continued, "Is there a reason why you don't ever invite them here? Are you embarrassed about something?"

"No," Kody began. "You and Mom are great to have around. It's not that at all. I just haven't given it much thought, that's all."

"Do you think you could work out a study session here one day a week?"

"I don't see why not," Kody replied.

A silence fell between father and son. Then Kody ventured his own question. "Dad, have you ever gone to church?"

"No. I've never attended."

"Not even as a kid?"

"You know your Grandma and Grandpa McLaughlin, Son. They don't participate in any religion and never have. Besides, I've never really seen anything that would prove to me there is a God. To me, the idea of a God is a myth, passed on from generation to generation without any real explanation. It's sort of a Christian mythology."

"But what about faith?"

"Faith? Faith in what?"

"Faith in God?"

Michael shook his head. "I have faith in very few things, Son, and God isn't one of them."

"But why not?"

"Okay, here's what I really think. I believe a long time ago the idea of a God was created to encourage people to do the right thing, but as time went on the meaning of it got lost and now all you have is different denominations and TV preachers wanting your membership so they can get into your pocket. Religion is big business, and wherever there's a dollar to be made shady characters abound. Some people will buy anything from anybody, including their so-called salvation."

Kody was quiet for a moment. Then he spoke. "Dad, I'm going to tell you something I think you won't like. I'm going to start taking the missionary lessons from the Mormon church."

Michael sucked in his breath but said nothing.

Kody continued, "You and Mom gave your permission for me to see this through to the end, and this is really important to me."

"But to what end, Kody? Are you going to join this religion?"

Suddenly the possibility of becoming a Mormon overwhelmed Kody. "I haven't thought about it," he said. "I'm not real sure."

"Kody, let me ask you something. What is missing in your young life that would make you cling to other people?"

Kody stared at his dad, confused. "What do you mean?"

"I mean, Jimmy Lee, Reanna, and their families. You're absorbing everything about them, including their religion. Why?"

"Oh, Dad, my interest in Mormons isn't because of Jimmy Lee and Reanna. I admit, I admire them a lot, but I really want to find out for myself whether or not there's a God, and this seems to be the best way."

Michael was silent for a moment. Then he asked, "When do these missionary meetings begin?"

"Wednesday at six-thirty. Will you and Mom come?"

"Where are they being held?"

Kody hesitated. "Jimmy Lee's house."

Michael thought, quietly stroking his chin. "I can't speak for your mother but I'll go, Kody."

"Thanks, Dad. This means a lot to me."

"I can tell." Michael rose from the bed. "We'd better go talk to your mom." Kody stood and followed his father out of his room.

Vonnie stood in the kitchen, stirring a cheese sauce for the scalloped potatoes.

Michael said nothing, waiting for Kody to take the lead. He said nervously, "Mom, I've talked to Dad and there's something I need to ask you."

Vonnie took the sauce off the burner and looked intently at her son.

"I've made an appointment with two missionaries from the Mormon church and we're going to have our first meeting on Wednesday evening. Dad said he'd come and I'd really like it if you'd come too."

Vonnie clenched her jaw and said nothing. Then she asked tightly, "What are the details?"

"It's going to be at six-thirty at Jimmy Lee's house."

"Why didn't you schedule it here?"

"I wasn't sure how you and Dad would feel about that."

"Did it ever occur to you to ask before you made the appointment?"

"Actually, it all happened so fast, I—"

"Kody, are they pushing you to do this?"

"No, Mom. That's not what I meant. I'm sorry. I should've asked first, I guess, but when you and Dad said I could explore this, I believed you were giving me permission for this kind of thing."

Vonnie nodded. "You're right about that. I don't want you to ever look back and blame us for holding you back. But I owe it to you, Kody, to let you know how I feel, and I don't like this. Not one bit. I see this church taking you away from your family, and I can't believe you would choose some religion over your own parents."

"It's not like that, Mom. I want you to come with me."

Vonnie was silent for a minute, then she nodded. "Okay, I'll go with you and meet the Donovans. Will Reanna and her family attend?"

"I don't know. Reanna probably will."

"Did your father talk to you about having your friends come over here once in a while?"

"Yes. Do you still want them to come over?"

"Of course. I hope they will."

"I'll set something up tomorrow. I'm sure they'll want to come."

Vonnie put the cheese sauce back on the burner and gave it her attention. Kody knew he was being dismissed. He gave his dad a hopeful look. His dad didn't say anything. Kody silently went back to his room.

Once again he picked up the sturdy little book and began to read. Already Kody was beginning to realize that a relationship with God would take some work. Even Nephi, who was considered to be a great prophet, had to work hard to learn many things. And then after Nephi did learn what he sought after, he bore the responsibility of sharing it with his two doubting brothers. Didn't Kody carry the same responsibility? Did he want the responsibility? If he had the great knowledge and faith of Nephi, wouldn't he want to share it with others? Wouldn't he want to share it with his family? Kody thought about the scripture he had just read in 1 Nephi chapter 2:19. *"Blessed art thou, Nephi, because of thy faith, for thou hast sought me diligently, with lowliness of heart."*

Could he, Kody, be likened to Nephi because he was seeking the Lord diligently? The question warmed him.

Kody was brought back to the present by his mother's voice calling from the kitchen. Dinnertime. Suddenly Kody realized he was famished.

CHAPTER 15

The following Wednesday Kody sat in the back of the family sedan and tried to swallow, but his mouth was too dry. The idea of missionary lessons made him nervous enough, but when he thought of his skeptical parents sitting with him he really became jittery. He knew the Donovans would be gracious and kind and his folks would respond in the same manner, but what if they totally rejected the message of the missionaries?

"Next left, Dad," he said. His voice croaked.

A few minutes later Michael turned into the Donovans' driveway. Kody recognized Reanna's car. Had the elders arrived?

Kody looked over his parents as they walked up the front porch. His father looked good in a pair of jeans and long-sleeved blue sweatshirt. His mom was wearing a tailored maroon suit with a soft pink blouse. She looked very professional but a little tired.

Taking a deep breath, Kody knocked on the door. Jimmy Lee answered it, her eyes lighting up. She wasn't the only one who greeted them at the door. Clover tumbled out of the house with tail wagging and jumped at Kody's feet. Immediately Kody felt better.

Opening the door wide, Jimmy Lee grinned. "Sorry," she said as she scooped up Clover. "She thinks everyone comes here to see her. I'm so glad you guys could make it," she said to Kody's parents. "I know how much this means to Kody." She stood aside. "Come on in."

Kody rubbed the puppy's ears. "So, this is Clover," he said. Clover tried to lick his hand.

Michael ushered Vonnie and Kody in first and then stood behind his family in the entryway. Suddenly Kody was grateful his parents had decided to support him with their attendance. It felt good to have them standing beside him. Kody could feel his father's hand resting on his shoulder and it made the daunting task of discovery a little easier.

Beth Donovan came in from the kitchen with Wes, wiping her hands on her apron. She held out her hand to Kody's parents. Jimmy Lee performed the introductions. "I'm so glad you could all come," Beth said warmly. She motioned toward the sofa. "Sit down. Would you like some hot chocolate? We don't drink coffee, but there's herbal tea if you'd rather."

Kody nodded. "Yes, please."

Vonnie shook her head. "No, thanks."

Michael smiled. "We're fine, thanks."

The doorbell rang again. It was the two elders. Kody introduced them to his parents and, with a steaming mug of hot chocolate, settled in between his mom and dad.

As the lesson got under way, Kody listened carefully. First Elder Young, then Elder Moore, talked of Joseph Smith, the First Vision, the Apostasy, the need for authority, and the restoration. It was all so new and foreign to Kody that he could hardly absorb it. But he listened hard, answering the questions thoughtfully. A couple of times the missionaries asked his father a question, but he just shook his head and gestured toward Kody. After it was over, Kody looked at his mom and dad. He couldn't read them. They had their company faces on.

They relaxed as Beth passed around fragrant gingerbread and whipped cream. Kody felt right at home as the conversation became general. His mother asked Elder Moore about his mission: How long would he teach? Could he communicate with his family? What did his parents think of his decision to leave his home in Colorado? What about his college education?

Michael was talking to Wes Donovan about the recent school board decisions to beef up the foreign language requirement.

Wes asked easily, "Do any of you have any questions about the lesson tonight?"

Kody looked at his folks.

"No. I think it was very self-explanatory," said Michael. "We'll go home and talk about it."

"You're welcome to attend any of our church meetings with Kody," Wes said, looking directly at Vonnie and Michael. "I hope you know that."

Vonnie smiled, but Kody knew that smile. It was her work smile. "Thank you. We'll let you know." She glanced at her watch. "We should be going, though. Kody still has some homework and oboe practice."

Kody reluctantly placed his mug and plate in the sink, and with a final pat for Clover he obediently followed his parents to the car. The drive was silent. Too silent. He wished he knew what they were thinking.

"Well, what do you think?" he finally asked.

"What you think is what really matters, Kody," Vonnie said.

Kody thought for a moment, hoping to choose his words carefully. "Well, it certainly is different. I'm looking forward to reading more in the Book of Mormon. I didn't know it came from gold plates."

Vonnie turned around and looked intently at her son. "Do you believe that?"

Kody blinked. "I don't disbelieve it," he said noncommittally. "I just want to explore and see if it's true, and the only way to do that is to do what the elders suggest. Read the Book of Mormon and pray."

"How long have you had a Book of Mormon?" Michael asked.

"I got a copy on Sunday."

"Why didn't you tell us?"

"I don't know. I thought about it, but you both seemed pretty upset already and I guess I didn't want to irritate the situation. Besides, we were talking about having Jimmy Lee and Reanna over one day this week, and the book just slipped my mind. Reanna and Jimmy Lee are planning on coming over tomorrow. You still want them to study at the house, don't you?"

Vonnie sighed. "Yes, of course, Kody." She turned and faced her son again. "I'm going to be completely honest with you, Kody. The Donovans seem very nice and I can see why you feel drawn to them. They're warm and appear to be loving and gracious, but I don't believe this Joseph Smith story for one minute. I think he snookered a bunch of people, and now this church has been created to justify his odd claims."

"But Mom, how can you know without reading and praying?"

"I don't have to read anything or pray to know when I'm being told a fish story."

Kody's heart plummeted. How could his mother deny everything after just one lesson? There was still so much to learn and understand.

"Will you go to church with me on Sunday? Maybe that will help you—"

"I don't need any help," Vonnie snapped. She forced out a long breath. "I'm sorry, Kody. I didn't mean to get cross. But the answer is no. I won't go to church with you and my original request stands. I hope you won't let this become so important that you neglect your family. I hope you'll choose to spend Sunday with us. Jimmy Lee and Reanna are always welcome at the house. They're good girls and they come from good families. That's obvious. We have given our permission when it comes to exploring their faith, and it wouldn't be fair of us to deny you that now; but I hope in the end, Kody, you'll reject the Mormon religion. I can't imagine what it must be like for the families of those two young men. Sending them out to Oregon without so much as an address. Do you know when a missionary is transferred to another area he's not allowed to call and tell his folks? Why, a couple of weeks could go by before they find him again. He can only call home on Mother's Day and Christmas."

"But, Mom, these young men choose to serve, and their families are proud of the choices they're making."

Vonnie's eyes filled with tears. "College is bad enough, but to send my son out for two years without so much as a phone call would be unthinkable. Some of them go to foreign countries!"

"Now, Von," Michael said gently as he placed his hand on his wife's knee. "Let's not get ahead of ourselves. Kody's only had one lesson."

Vonnie choked back her tears and swallowed hard. She placed her hand over her husband's. "You're right, Michael," she said gently. "But it doesn't change my mind." She looked directly at Kody. "You have my permission to explore, Kody, but in the end, I hope you'll turn away from a religion that would demand so much of you and be so willing to take you away from your family."

Kody looked down at his lap. "Mom, I know I don't have any answers. All I can tell you is that when I'm around Reanna and Jimmy Lee I feel warm inside. I get that same feeling when I attend church, and last Sunday when I read the Book of Mormon for the first time, I felt it again."

"What kind of a feeling?" Michael asked.

Kody thought for a moment. "Like I'm on the edge of a wonderful discovery."

"Maybe it's not Mormonism you're so enamored with. Maybe it's Jimmy Lee and Reanna. They're very charismatic girls. Have you thought about that?" Vonnie asked.

"Yes, Mom, I have; and I won't deny that Reanna and Jimmy Lee are who made me curious but they're not responsible for the rest of my feelings."

"Well, I'm not completely convinced of that, Kody," Vonnie said.

Kody nodded but said nothing.

At home, Kody thanked his parents for attending the discussion, then headed into his room to finish his homework. But as he studied calculus the little book beckoned to him; and after he had finished with his homework he pulled it down from the shelf and almost immediately became engrossed.

Then he remembered what the elders had asked him to do. For the first time in his life, Kody got down on his knees and began a prayer. It was halting and awkward and no answer came, but Kody wasn't discouraged. Relationships took time, and if there truly was a God—and he was beginning to believe there was—then Kody expected it would take some time to get acquainted.

CHAPTER 16

The following Monday, Kody sat in Mr. Svenson's studio and carefully went through his arpeggios. Mr. Svenson listened intently. "Watch the high A, Kody," he said. "It's always flat and you're not giving it enough support."

Kody played high A again and forced more air into his oboe. The pitch rose.

Mr. Svenson nodded. "Yes. Perfect. Tell me, Kody, how have your practice sessions been going?"

Kody sighed. "Okay, I guess."

Mr. Svenson raised his eyebrows.

"Well, it depends. Some days are okay, but other days are not so good. I don't see why it matters *how* I play as long as I get the notes right. I mean, no one can tell what I'm thinking. Maybe I'm thinking about my friends but maybe I'm thinking about a crater on the moon. Why should it matter?"

"It matters because a crater on the moon would evoke a different response in those listening. Not a bad response, just different." Mr. Svenson rummaged through Kody's music and pulled out the Vivaldi piece Kody had played often. "Play a crater on the moon," he said.

Kody looked at the music. It was a light happy piece. "But this isn't moon crater music," he said.

"If this isn't moon crater music, then what kind of music is it?"

"It's friend music," Kody said thoughtfully.

"Yes." Mr. Svenson pulled out another piece. "What kind of feelings would you want this piece to evoke?"

Kody looked over the familiar Bach Wedding Cantata. "Weddings are usually happy affairs, so you'd want this to be happy."

Mr. Svenson pulled out more music. "What about this one?"

"Well, it depends on which movement you're playing. The second movement sounds kind of like a funeral."

"Okay. So I want you to play a funeral."

Kody picked up his oboe and played.

Mr. Svenson shook his head. "No. There's no swelling of the phrase. No sadness. Make your oboe cry."

Kody wasn't sure how to proceed.

Mr. Svenson continued. "Kody, have you ever been to a funeral?"

Kody shook his head.

"I'm going to tell you a story, Kody. Many years ago I had a dear friend who lost his four-year-old daughter. She was hit by a car. My friend asked me to play at his daughter's funeral and I chose this piece." He picked up his oboe and played the first two lines. "Do you hear the difference? I infused my emotion into the song. I interpreted the music as a sad, mournful piece and that's what I played. You try."

Kody began again. He tried to picture grieving parents. Slowly the music ebbed out of him. He quit halfway through the piece. "But couldn't it sound a bit triumphant?" he asked.

Mr. Svenson looked at his pupil. "Explain what you mean."

"I'm not sure," Kody said slowly. "Maybe I'm wrong."

"No. No, you're not wrong. Continue with your thought."

"I'm just thinking that if you gave it a strong finish, maybe it would bring hope instead of despair. You see, I'm learning about a new religion and I'm beginning to believe that there's life after death."

"So, you don't see this piece as despondent?"

"I don't think it has to be."

Mr. Svenson smiled. "Perfect. Kody, you've just interpreted a piece of music. You didn't copy me or my thoughts. You came up with your own ideas and so you'll play it with your own unique angle. Play the whole thing."

With new resolve, Kody once again visualized grieving parents. The music started softly and with reverence. Then he began to build in momentum. Gradually he pushed the tempo and volume until the music was intense. The last note rang clear, strong, and determined.

Mr. Svenson nodded thoughtfully. "Yes, you could do it like that." He picked up his oboe and played the last two lines. But instead of playing them with intensity, he played them quietly. "Do you hear a difference?"

"Oh, yes," Kody said.

"Does it evoke a different feeling?"

"Yes."

"The same notes, Kody. Just played with different thoughts. When I played this movement for my friend and his wife, I wanted to give them a moment of peace. I felt this was the best way to do it. You approached the same music wanting to impart triumph and hope, so you played it differently. That's what music is about. Creating pictures and feelings inside of people. Inside yourself."

"Now," Mr. Svenson asked, "how does this new religion make you feel?"

"It makes me feel warm inside. It draws me in and invites me to explore. It feels like I'm discovering treasure."

"Okay. I want you to pick out a piece of music and I want you to play treasure for me."

Kody looked through his music and picked out a Haydn concerto. He thumbed through the pages until he found the movement he was seeking. He placed it on the stand, and with new zeal he played the piece. It was rough. He made mistakes. Frustrated, he quit playing. "This isn't right," he said.

"Why not?" Mr. Svenson asked.

"This piece is familiar to me. I shouldn't be making these mistakes."

"Be patient with yourself, Kody. Yes, you've played this piece many times, but you haven't ever played it with feelings before. Playing musically takes just as much effort as playing the correct notes. For the next week, I'd like for you to play this piece again. You know the notes, so concentrate on making it sound like treasure."

Kody nodded and began putting his instrument away.

"By the way, what is this new religion that has captured your interest?"

"The Church of Jesus Christ of Latter-day Saints. They're often called Mormons."

"Ah, yes. I've heard of Mormons. Are your new friends Mormons?"

Kody nodded. "Both Jimmy Lee and Reanna belong to the Church."

"Well, Kody, I wish you luck in your discovery of treasure."

"Thank you, Mr. Svenson." Kody rose from his chair.

CHAPTER 17

Jimmy Lee sat alone in her backyard and watched the sun filter through the maple branches. The sun offered warmth and promised more. New sprigs of green grass were beginning to show.

She walked to the flower beds and studied them. Already she could see new green sprigs reaching for the light of the sun. She smiled. It was a good thing she had finished the weeding. Now her precious flowers could grow unhindered.

Clover was tugging at her cowboy boots. Jimmy Lee pushed the puppy away. "No!" she said sharply. Clover looked dejected, but as soon as Jimmy Lee bent down to peer at the new bulbs, Clover began trying to crawl into her lap.

Jimmy Lee laughed and picked up the puppy, even though her paws were muddy. She continued to study the bulbs, naming the flowers; crocus, they would bloom first; daffodils, tulips, lilies . . . Yes, lilies. Jimmy Lee looked into her favorite corner of the flower plot. Tiny little shoots were showing themselves. Her Easter lilies would be blooming soon. Last year she had neglected them. They had bloomed without her care, and Jimmy Lee had felt bad that she hadn't even gone out once to admire her favorite gift of nature. She had been too busy with Mitch and their activities to show any appreciation for her beloved lilies.

Not this time! Jimmy Lee looked forward to their flower and she remembered the story her mother told her every year on Easter Sunday.

One of Jimmy Lee's earliest memories was of Easter morning. She had just awakened to find a basket of candy with a white stuffed rabbit sitting on her nightstand. A present from the Easter bunny. She had been delighted in the gift and hurriedly opened the cellophane to check the goodies.

"No candy before church," Beth said from the door.

Jimmy Lee looked up to see her mother carrying the most beautiful flower she had ever seen. She put the candy back in the basket. "What's that?" she asked.

"This is called an Easter lily, and your father and I bought it for you. This plant has very special meaning." Beth sat on the bed. "See how these flowers are formed? They kind of look like a bell or a trumpet, don't they?"

Jimmy Lee nodded.

"This is to remind us of when Jesus comes back on the earth," Beth explained. Then she asked, "What color are these flowers, Jimmy Lee?"

"They're white."

"Yes. They also stand for the purity of Jesus, because He lived on this earth without making any mistakes."

Jimmy Lee squirmed in her bed. "I wish I could be like Jesus," she said.

Beth put her arm around her young daughter. "Someday you'll be like Jesus, but you have to try hard to be a good girl, and remember to say you're sorry when you make mistakes."

Jimmy Lee was comforted by her mother's words and she snuggled against her.

As years went by, Jimmy Lee learned other things about the Easter lily. It was the first lily to bloom in the spring, signifying the firstborn of God. It always died back after a few weeks but every year it renewed itself, reminding her of the important gift her Savior had offered to all mankind, the gift of eternal life.

As Jimmy Lee grew older, she came to anticipate the lily her mother would bring into her room every year. It became more important than the candy. Then when Jimmy Lee was eleven, her parents decided to quit giving her the flowers. They had transplanted all ten lilies into their yard and they scarcely had room for more. At first Jimmy Lee was disappointed, but then she found that her anticipation grew as she waited for ten lily plants to bloom.

Now that she was in high school, the lilies meant even more to her. They represented faith. Faith in Jesus and faith in her Heavenly Father. Once again she thought of the scripture that had captured her attention. *"Consider the lilies of the field . . ."* Where could she find that scripture?

Balancing Clover on her hip, Jimmy Lee wiped the dog's paws before hurrying to her room. She pulled out her Bible and looked in the Topical Guide. She found the scripture in several places, but her favorite was in Doctrine and Covenants 84:82–83. Yes! It made perfect sense. If her Father in Heaven was willing to clothe the lilies of the field in beauty and splendor, then wouldn't He take care of her? Hadn't He been taking care of her all along?

Humility washed through her. But still some stubborn little part of her heart was not ready to let go. "No," she thought desperately. "I'm not ready to give up on Mitch yet." Tears spilled onto her cheeks. Things would never be as they were before. For weeks now that had been her hope and prayer; that he would tire of Brenda and make his way back to her. But as winter eventually turned to spring, she knew things could never be the same. Not because of Mitch, but because she had changed.

Hugging her Bible close, Jimmy Lee whispered a silent prayer of thanks for her new ability to understand the recent events, which were shaping her life. She was not forgotten, neither was she alone.

CHAPTER 18

The following Thursday, Jimmy Lee sat on the steps of the main school building waiting for Reanna. The air had a hint of warmth and the sun beamed clear.

Jimmy Lee really appreciated the ride home, but she never knew how long she would have to wait for Reanna. There was always a line of boys waiting to talk to her popular friend, or possibly get a date. Especially now that the spring dance was coming up, the troops had swelled in numbers. It was going to be a long wait.

Sighing, Jimmy Lee opened her geometry book and began studying the equations in her next assignment. She liked math and was so engrossed in the problems that she didn't even see or hear Rick Morris sit beside her on the steps. Finally he cleared his throat. Jimmy Lee looked up.

"Oh, hi, Rick. What's up?" she asked, closing her book, her finger marking the page.

Rick shaded his blue eyes and looked out over the parking lot. His blond hair ruffled in the slight breeze. "Not much. How about you?"

Jimmy Lee shrugged. "Just working on some geometry."

The young man nodded and then looked at Jimmy Lee. "Um, I was wondering," he hesitated. "I was wondering if you'd want to go see a movie or something this Friday night."

Jimmy Lee blinked. A date? A real date? "A movie sounds good," she replied, giving him her best smile.

Rick visibly relaxed. "Good. How about I pick you up at six-thirty."

"Fine."

He stood to go. "Well, I should get home. I'll see you Friday night." He sauntered down the steps toward his car.

Jimmy Lee watched him walk out of sight. A pleasant feeling stirred within. Rick Morris was not exactly every girl's dream, like Mitch. He was on the track team, lean of build, and a better-than-average student. Jimmy Lee had always liked Rick as a friend. Maybe this could be the start of something good. Maybe Jimmy Lee could even learn how to play the field as Reanna kept advising her to do. She smiled just before Reanna came bounding down the stairs.

"Sorry to keep you waiting," Reanna said breathlessly.

"You say that every day," Jimmy Lee replied.

"I know. I know. Hey, what did Rick have to say? I saw him sitting by you for a few minutes."

"He asked me out for Friday night." Jimmy Lee grinned.

Reanna's face lit up. "Oh, Jimmy Lee, that's great. Rick is such a nice guy. You'll have a great time."

"Have you ever gone out with him?"

Reanna shook her head. "No. He's never asked me."

"Well, that's a first." Jimmy Lee pretended shock. "He's the only boy in the whole school who hasn't asked you out, but he's probably dreamed of it."

"Don't be so sure," Reanna said. They climbed into her car. "Hey, what did you think of Kody's missionary lesson last night?" Reanna asked as she pulled into the traffic.

"I thought it went very well. It was only his second lesson and I can feel that he's really serious about this. He was very responsive and really paid attention. His dad seems to absorb the information, too, but it's obvious that he's more neutral than Kody."

"It's too bad his mother didn't come," Reanna commented. Then she continued. "I was impressed with how much he's read from the Book of Mormon. He really seems sincere."

Jimmy Lee became thoughtful. "You know, it's odd how something so basic to my life isn't even a part of Kody's. I mean, my belief in God has always been there. From the time I was a small child, I remember knowing about Heavenly Father and Jesus. It's hard to imagine having to learn all those things at our age." She paused. "Do you think he'll be baptized?"

Reanna thought for a moment. "I wish I could say yes, but I'm not sure. He seems enthusiastic but he never discusses baptism. When the elders try to give him the baptismal challenge, he always says, 'Right now, I'm just learning.' "

Reanna changed the subject as she pulled into Jimmy Lee's driveway. "I'm excited about your date Friday night. It should be fun."

"Who are you going out with this weekend?" Jimmy Lee asked.

"Eric Miller," Reanna said with a dreamy look in her eyes.

"He doesn't even go to our school."

"I know, but he's in our stake and I've always kind of admired him." She giggled.

"Well, don't forget about our study session with Kody later this evening."

"I'll be here to pick you up around six-thirty."

Later that same evening Kody sat at the dining room table with Jimmy Lee and Reanna. They were diligently studying their personal finance assignment. Each student was required to keep a budget on a certain amount of funds. It had been an ongoing project since the beginning of the semester. As they compared notes now, weeks into the semester, they found their spending habits fascinating.

Kody was looking through Jimmy Lee and Reanna's mock checkbooks. "What's this?" he asked, pointing at an entry in Reanna's register written for $140 to the Diamond Soul Shoe Store.

"I needed new shoes," Reanna said casually.

"New shoes!" Kody laughed. "Where's your grocery money?" He flipped back through the register. "You haven't bought groceries in over a month. What do you plan to eat?"

Reanna shrugged. "Jimmy Lee will feed me," she said with an air of certainty.

Jimmy Lee looked at Reanna sharply. "Yeah. I'll cut up those new leather shoes and pour a little steak sauce on them."

The three laughed. Kody began looking through Jimmy Lee's register. "What's this?" he asked. "Fifty dollars made out to Glendale Ward."

"That's my tithing," Jimmy Lee answered.

Kody was glad his folks were in the family room, watching television. "What's tithing?"

"The Church asks members to give 10 percent of their gross income to the Church," she explained.

Kody stared at her in shock. "Ten percent? That could be a lot of money." Suddenly, his father's words came rushing back. Could it be that Christianity really was nothing more than big business? He became suspicious. "Why didn't anybody tell me about this?"

"You've only had two missionary discussions, Kody. I'm sure it'll be discussed soon," Reanna said.

"Do your folks give 10 percent?"

Both girls nodded.

"And how about you Reenie? You have a real job. Do you give 10 percent of your gross income?"

She nodded. "Yes, I do. Why are you so perplexed by this? We don't pass the collection plate during services, like some denominations. Where do you think our meetinghouses and our temples come from? Those things have to be financed."

"Really, Kody," Jimmy Lee interrupted. "It's all about discipline. In the scriptures we're told we need to be thankful to the Lord for all He gives us. It's also a reminder that we need to love our Heavenly Father first and not replace Him with money."

"But you're not giving the money to God," Kody argued. "You're giving it to an organization."

"The Church isn't just any organization. It's the true Church of the living God," Jimmy Lee pointed out.

"Even the Bible tells us about tithing," Reanna said.

"That's right," Jimmy Lee affirmed.

"Where?" Kody asked.

The two girls looked at each other. "We don't know right off, but we'll find them for you and let you know on Sunday," Reanna said confidently.

Kody backed down a little. "Okay," he said.

"Now, let me see how you spend your nickels and dimes," Jimmy Lee said as she pulled Kody's papers out from underneath his arm. "Hmmmm. Ten dollars for hot rod magazines. Forty dollars for music? I didn't realize how expensive music could be."

"That was only two books. A Kalliwoda concerto and a Cimarosa concerto. Oh, and I bought a book of études too."

"What are études?" Jimmy Lee asked.

"A book of practice pieces."

"Could you play them for us?" Reanna asked excitedly.

"Etudes? Most of them aren't really something to listen to."

"Okay, how about one of the other pieces?" Reanna asked.

"Yeah, Kody, could you?" Jimmy Lee asked.

"I-I don't know," Kody stammered. "I don't know these pieces very well." Once again Kody thought about Mr. Svenson. His teacher had encouraged Kody to buy the new pieces of music and interpret them before his next lesson. It had been slow going, and Kody wondered if he was on the right track. He was still working on the Haydn piece. His treasure music.

Reanna interrupted Kody's thoughts. "Well, I'm sure you've got other music, you know. We'd love to hear you play, wouldn't we Jimmy Lee?"

Jimmy Lee nodded enthusiastically. "Please, Kody?"

Kody grinned. "Well, all right, if you're sure you won't be bored."

"We promise," both girls said in unison.

A few minutes later Kody appeared with his oboe, music, and stand. He set everything up. "First, I need to warm up, then I'll play a solo written by Vivaldi. I've been working on this for a while."

For a brief moment Kody closed his eyes and remembered Mr. Svenson's words about playing from the heart. This was the piece that had reminded Kody of his two friends because of its upbeat and light tune. Now, with Reanna and Jimmy Lee sitting in front of him, it became easier to express that happiness through the notes.

The girls were spellbound as Kody played a melody neither of them had heard before.

After he was finished, both girls looked at him in awe. "Kody," Reanna said, her eyes wide. "That was beautiful."

"You sure paint beautiful pictures, Kody," Jimmy Lee said.

"What do you mean?" Kody asked.

"I mean, I could almost picture a gurgling stream in a forest on a mild summer day. It's such a sweet and happy tune."

Kody caught his breath. Was this what Mr. Svenson was talking about? Could he possibly have the power to paint pictures in the minds of those who listened to his music? The thought was almost overwhelming.

Jimmy Lee became excited. "Kody? Could you play lilies for me?"

Kody blinked. "Lilies?"

"Yes. Could you find a song that reminds you of lilies in a meadow with butterflies? I love lilies. They're my favorite flower."

"Since when have you loved lilies?" Reanna asked.

"I've always loved lilies, Reenie. Just the other day I found a beautiful scripture in the Bible. It talks about the lilies of the field and how God knows and understands our needs."

Kody looked through his music. Nothing there reminded him of lilies. Maybe it was because he was so taken aback by Jimmy Lee's request. Finally he pulled out a movement from a Mozart concerto. "Maybe this is it," he said.

Placing the music on the stand, Kody tried to picture lilies, but he wasn't sure what they looked like. Slowly he tried to play the music, but it didn't sound right. Disappointment crowded into his heart. He stopped. "I'm sorry. I guess I'm not quite sure what a lily looks like."

"It kind of looks like the bottom of your oboe," Jimmy Lee said. "It's a bell-shaped flower, and they come in all colors, but Easter lilies are my favorite. They're pure white and are the first lily to bloom in the spring."

Kody tried again, but the music still didn't work. "I don't think I can play lilies," he said.

Reanna jumped in. "That's okay. I like happier songs, myself. Can you play another happy tune?"

Kody went through his music once again and played another melody. It sounded better.

Vonnie McLaughlin appeared in the doorway, smiling at her son. "I thought I heard your oboe, Kody. You girls should come to Kody's next recital."

"We'd love to come," Jimmy Lee said. "Could you play us another one?"

"Maybe one more," he said, then launched into a short tune.

"You should play in church, someday," Jimmy Lee suggested. "They'd love you."

"Oh, I don't know," Kody said.

Vonnie stepped inside. "You mean, Kody would be allowed to play during one of your meetings?"

"Absolutely!" Jimmy Lee said. "He could play during sacrament meeting."

"We could talk to the music director," Reanna chimed in. "He's our seminary teacher, so it shouldn't be hard to catch him."

"I'd need someone to play the piano for me," Kody hedged.

"Oh, that wouldn't be any problem," Reanna said. "There's lots of piano players in church."

"But would they be willing to spend time with me, working on the music?"

"Sure. People in our ward do it all the time, don't they, Jimmy Lee?"

Jimmy Lee nodded in agreement.

"Why, Kody, that might be fun," Vonnie said. "It'd be a bigger group than you're used to in your recitals."

Reanna was excited. "Boy, Kody, I'd say you're the school's best-kept secret."

Kody warmed under the praise. "Thanks, Reanna."

A few minutes later, Kody walked the girls to Reanna's car. "Maybe we should get together tomorrow night," he suggested. "We could catch a movie or something."

Reanna and Jimmy Lee looked at each other. Then Jimmy Lee said, "Kody, Rick and I are going to a movie. It's my first date since breaking up with Mitch."

"Oh," Kody replied, understanding the importance of Jimmy Lee's words. He looked hopefully at Reanna.

"And I'm going out with someone too," Reanna added.

Kody's heart sank. "Well, maybe sometime next week," he said, sounding more cheerful than he felt.

"We'll see you on Sunday, though, won't we?" Reanna asked.

"I'll be there," Kody answered. He waved the girls out of the driveway.

Looking up at the sky, he noticed the stars were covered by a blanket of clouds. No word from the heavens tonight. But if there really was a God, then it wouldn't matter if the stars were covered. God would still be able to find a way to communicate, if He wanted to. Kody stood quietly in the driveway, listening to the night sounds of the neighborhood and gazing at the blank sky above, waiting for a message. None came.

Tithing. He wondered what Reanna and Jimmy Lee would have to say about it on Sunday. He wondered whether maybe his parents had been right all along.

He thought about the first time he had stared into the starry sky. Had that warmth been a product of his imagination? No. Deep down, Kody knew it was real. A power greater than he had acknowledged his gratitude. Someone was there. Instead of looking into the night sky and asking if there was a God, Kody looked into the cloudy heavens and said, "There is a God," his voice low and soft.

Unmistakably, then, Kody was filled with a certainty of his last statement. He was awestruck by the power bursting forth from him. *"There is a God!"* he said, exultantly. The familiar warmth of discovery spread throughout his body, making him feel alive. Suddenly, Kody was filled with the desire to know more. What other truths lie waiting for him to search out?

He returned to the house. He knew what he needed to do. It wasn't the Lord who needed to find a way to communicate. It was Kody. He closed the door to his room and knelt beside his bed. All awkwardness disappeared; and for the first time in his life Kody truly prayed.

CHAPTER 19

Jimmy Lee looked in the mirror and swallowed hard. She wished Reanna was beside her, clucking and fussing and lecturing her on how to behave. Instead, Clover was tearing around the room with her new rope toy. Jimmy Lee stopped fussing and watched the puppy, who promptly ran into the bedpost. Jimmy Lee laughed and then picked up Clover to comfort her.

A soft knock sounded at the door. Her mother appeared with a crystal bottle in her hand. "This is my favorite fragrance," she said. "Your father bought it for me in Paris when we went there for our second honeymoon—you remember?"

That had been a couple of years ago. Jimmy Lee knew the bottle well. It stood on her mother's dresser and was used for special occasions.

"Only a little," Beth said. "Or you'll have to drive with the windows open," she giggled.

Jimmy Lee smiled. She was beginning to feel a little calmer. She put the puppy down, and with dainty motions she dabbed a little of the perfume on her wrists and throat before handing the crystal bottle back.

Beth stepped back to look at her daughter. "You look lovely, honey."

Even though this was a casual-dress date, Jimmy Lee had traded her usual wardrobe of cowboy boots and flannel shirts for cream-colored, lightweight corduroy pants, and a light blue cotton sweater. She looked delicate, softer.

Wes poked his head in the door. "Mmmm!" he exclaimed, then came in and kissed her on the cheek.

Allison joined the family. "Are you worried that Rick isn't a Mormon?" she asked.

Jimmy Lee shook her head. "No. Rick and I are just friends. I don't plan on getting serious with him. I won't make that mistake again."

Allison became still. "I think I hear his car." She raced out of the room and returned seconds later. "He just drove in!" she squealed.

Suddenly, Jimmy Lee felt flustered again. "I don't know why I'm so nervous," she said. "It's not like this is such a big deal."

"You're just not used to dating someone new," Beth said, giving her daughter a reassuring hug. "Don't worry. Everything will be fine."

The doorbell rang and Jimmy Lee's father held up his hand. "Don't come out," he instructed. "I have a few questions for this young man."

Jimmy Lee blushed. Mitch had managed to escape a formal interview by being the first boy she dated after turning sixteen, when her folks had been as new at dating as she.

She listened hard, shushing Clover whenever she tried to whine or yap. Did Rick smoke? Was he a drinker? What time would he be bringing Jimmy Lee home? Did he know that her curfew was midnight? Was there a number where they could be reached? What were his parents' names and his home phone number?

Jimmy Lee rolled her eyes heavenward. Beth giggled softly and squeezed her hand. "Don't you worry about Rick," she said. "He should be able to take it. Besides, it builds character."

Jimmy Lee heard her father come down the hall. "Jimmy Lee," he called. "Rick's here."

Jimmy Lee hurried from the room with Clover at her heels. Rick was sitting on the sofa. He looked a little stunned, she thought. "Hi, Rick," she said shyly.

He rose immediately. "Hi, Jimmy Lee. You really look nice."

She smiled. "Thanks."

"Who's this?" he asked, looking at the puppy.

"This is Clover. She's new to our family."

Clover bounded toward Rick and then stopped. She sniffed in Rick's general direction and took a couple of cautious steps toward him. Rick bent down and called to Clover, who lost all inhibitions and bounded toward him.

"She must smell my dog," Rick said as he began petting her. "She sure is cute." He began walking Jimmy Lee toward the door. Clover followed as if she were going on the date too. Beth picked her up and held her as Jimmy Lee called her good-byes.

Rick opened the passenger door. It was not the old, gray Nissan pickup with the bent fender he usually drove to school. This was a Chrysler New Yorker with plush burgundy interior and a CD player.

"I borrowed my parents' car," Rick said as he slowly pulled out of the drive. "I didn't know if you'd want to bounce around in that old pickup of mine."

"I like your pickup," Jimmy Lee said. Then she added hurriedly, "This is very nice, though."

A strained silence fell. She and Mitch had always been so comfortable together. From the very first evening they had seemed right for each other. Now, here she sat in an unfamiliar car that smelled like an air freshener, and she couldn't think of a thing to say. Finally, she blurted out, "Tell me about your dog."

Rick looked at her and smiled his well-known crooked grin. "Her name is Polar."

"Why Polar? That's an interesting name."

"She's a Great Pyrenees, and they're all white. They have a lot of hair, too. She has to be brushed every day."

"Is she big?"

"She's huge," Rick said with enthusiasm. "She weighs close to 130 pounds."

"I'd love to see her!" Jimmy Lee exclaimed.

"Okay. After the movie we can stop by my house, and I'll introduce you to my folks. Polar will enjoy meeting you too."

She couldn't stop herself from saying, "Will they give me the kind of interview you got tonight?"

They both laughed. Rick gasped, "I wasn't sure I was going to pass!"

Suddenly the tension was gone.

The movie was a fast-paced romantic thriller. Only when they were back in the car did Jimmy Lee realize that Rick hadn't even tried to hold her hand. A rush of gratitude for his tact enveloped her.

A few minutes later they pulled into a driveway in an up-scale neighborhood. Rick opened Jimmy Lee's door and immediately she heard a deep-throated bark.

"That's Polar," Rick grinned.

A couple of minutes later Jimmy Lee was meeting Rick's parents and looking into the brown eyes of the most beautiful dog she had ever seen. Her tail wagged like a ceiling fan and she energetically licked Jimmy Lee's hands and arms. Polar's white coat was silky and she was obviously well cared for.

"I bet this hair takes a lot of work," Jimmy Lee said from her position in front of Polar.

The Morris family exchanged looks. Mrs. Morris laughed. "Bath time around here can be a real circus."

After a few minutes Rick's parents excused themselves, and the evening turned into a romp. Jimmy Lee was impressed with how smart and well-trained Rick's furry companion was. She hoped Clover would one day be so well behaved.

Polar seemed delighted with the attention, nuzzling Jimmy Lee with instant affection. It was love at first sight.

After an hour Rick glanced at his watch. "I'd better get you home. I told your dad we'd be back by ten-thirty and it's about that time now."

Jimmy Lee stood up reluctantly. "Can we bring Polar with us?"

"Sure. If you don't mind bouncing around in my truck. My folks don't like the dog to ride in the car because of the hair." Rick fished in his pocket for his keys. Then he looked at Jimmy Lee with concern. "I guess I should've asked you this sooner, but you don't mind about your clothes getting all hairy, do you?" he asked.

Jimmy Lee laughed. "No, of course not."

Polar lay between them, her head on Rick's lap. Jimmy Lee was scrunched against the door, Polar's tail whacking her during enthusiastic moments. Rick tried to get the dog to sit up. Polar only licked Rick's hand and thrashed her tail wildly. "Sorry," he apologized. "She's not used to sharing the seat."

"That's okay," Jimmy Lee said. "I love Polar, even if all I get is her tail."

"You're crazy about dogs, aren't you?" Rick asked. "I remember—," he broke off and swiftly changed the subject. "How long have you had Clover?"

"A couple of weeks," Jimmy Lee said, grateful he hadn't mentioned Ruff. "She's a lot of fun. Do you think Polar and Clover could play together someday?"

"Sure. Polar has always been good with other dogs. She thinks all dogs are potential best friends and playmates."

Rick pulled into Jimmy Lee's driveway and walked her to the door. "Thanks for coming with me," he said, sounding shy again.

"Thanks for asking me. And thanks for introducing me to your family and to Polar. I really had a good time tonight."

"You did?" Rick asked.

Jimmy Lee could smell a faint doggy odor on her sweater, but she felt comfortable, even happy. "Yeah, I did."

With a gentle motion, Rick cupped Jimmy Lee's chin in his hand and kissed her softly on the mouth. His lips were warm and lingered for just a moment. Jimmy Lee was surprised at the warm invitation in Rick's kiss. She could feel herself blushing and was glad it was dark.

Rick backed away from Jimmy Lee. They could hear Polar

whining in the truck. "Well, I'll see you on Monday," he said. "Maybe we could do this again sometime soon."

"Sure, Rick. I'd like that," she said.

Her parents were watching television. Clover bounded up to Jimmy Lee and sniffed her for a good three minutes before she yapped excitedly.

"It must've taken her a minute to realize it was really me," Jimmy Lee said as she tickled the puppy. Clover responded by rolling around on the carpet and licking Jimmy Lee's hands.

"How did it go?" Beth asked, rising from the sofa. Wes followed them to the kitchen, where Jimmy Lee sat down in a cloud of dog hair.

"It was fun," she exclaimed. "The movie was great, and then Rick took me to his house and I met his folks and his dog."

"So you really did have a good time?" Wes asked.

Jimmy Lee smiled. "Yeah. I really did."

"Well, I'm bringing your bathrobe so you can change without walking on the carpet again," said Beth. Your clothes need to go straight into the washing machine, or I'll be vacuuming for a week." Beth shook her head. "I hope Clover doesn't get this hairy," she smiled.

Dressed in her bathrobe, Jimmy Lee went to her room. She looked around, puzzled. Something didn't feel right. Was it the lingering smell of Polar? No, it was—it was Mitch! The mementos and photos of their life together were beginning to feel intrusive. The girl she saw in those photos was no longer who she was. She was not the same person Mitch had dumped two months ago. She had branched out, cultivated new friendships, and nurtured old ones. Slowly she began to take down the framed photos, looking intently at each one. Sometimes the memories were happy and sometimes they would fill her heart with sorrow, but the painful, throbbing ache was gone. Without her awareness it had slowly disappeared, to be replaced by a quiet acceptance.

Slowly moving to her dresser, Jimmy Lee fingered the prom picture. Her red satin dress burned the color of mute coals under the lights, and Mitch looked handsome and manly in his black tux. But once again her eyes were drawn to Ruff. The big black dog with his red bow tie and doggie grin fit right in. Oh, how Jimmy Lee missed Ruff! Surprised, she realized she missed Ruff more than she missed Mitch! On one particular date when she was feeling silly, she had smothered the dog with kisses. Ruff loved the attention, and Mitch shook her hand at the door that night instead of giving her the usual good-night kiss.

Jimmy Lee laughed, then half-caught her breath on a sob. How stupid to get sentimental over Mitch's dog!

Quietly she reached for Clover, who was just settling down at the foot of the bed. The dog gave a sleepy yawn and then licked Jimmy Lee's hand before settling back to sleep. Her warm soft body comforted Jimmy Lee.

A soft knock sounded at the door. "I heard a lot of commotion going on in here and I just wanted to make sure everything was all right," Beth said.

"Oh, Mom, I'm fine. I'm just cleaning some of this stuff out."

"I see that." Beth perched on Jimmy Lee's bed.

"You know, Mom," Jimmy Lee began. "Sometimes I miss Ruff."

Beth gave her a strange look.

"I mean, I really loved Mitch's dog. He was a good friend to me, and I wonder if he misses me. Do you think dogs know when something has changed?"

Beth thought for a moment. "Well, I don't think they are aware of it on the same level humans are, but I'm sure they can sense when things are different. Remember how Clover responded to Rick? She knew something was different."

Jimmy Lee laughed at the memory and then grew somber. "I wonder if Ruff likes Brenda Timmins," she said, wrinkling her nose.

"Well, now, that would probably depend on whether or not Brenda Timmins likes him. Are they still together? From what you told me about the basketball game, it sounded like they had a terrible quarrel and broke up."

Jimmy Lee shrugged. "Apparently Brenda forgave him, because they were glued to each other on Monday."

"How are you feeling about putting these things away?" Beth gestured toward the pile of pictures, the baseball cap, and other memorabilia that tracked Jimmy Lee's life with Mitch.

Jimmy Lee sighed as she stroked Clover. "It feels like it's time to put it away. I'm not the same person I was two months ago. Too much has happened."

"Yes. You really have grown up, Jimmy Lee. You've faced some difficult decisions and your father and I are very proud of the way you've handled them." Beth smiled and hugged her daughter close.

CHAPTER 20

"So how did your date go with Rick?" Reanna asked over the phone.

"I had a lot of fun," Jimmy Lee answered. "We went to the movies, and then he took me home and I met his folks and his dog."

"His dog?"

"Yeah. He has this beautiful white dog. She's a Great Pyrenees and she's huge. Anyway, he calls her Polar, and I really like her."

"What did Clover think of her?" Reanna asked.

"She didn't meet Polar, but she sure sniffed me over when I came home. She sniffed Rick over too. I think he had to meet with her approval before I could go out with him. It was kind of funny. He passed both Clover's test and my dad's test too."

"Your dad's test? Don't tell me your dad interviewed Rick."

"Yeah."

"My dad does that every time. I'm surprised anyone will ask me out anymore. It's like passing some ritual. I bet I know all the questions. Your dad has probably been talking to my dad."

Jimmy Lee laughed.

"Would you go out with Rick again, if he asks?" Reanna asked.

"Yeah, I would. In fact, I'd really like to get together so that our dogs could play. And you know what else? I'd go out with someone else too. I mean, it felt really good to be out with Rick. At first I was uncomfortable and I didn't know what to say, but after a while I began to feel better, and it was fun. How did your date with Eric go?"

"Oh, Jimmy Lee, I had the best time. Eric is wonderful," Reanna crooned.

Jimmy Lee was alarmed. She couldn't remember Reanna ever sounding so breathless over a boy before. Usually she just went out to have a good time.

"He asked me to the spring dance and I said yes," Reanna said.

"He doesn't even go to our school. How does he know about the spring dance?"

"I don't know," Reanna answered, "but I don't care. I'm just so excited about him being my escort. Do you think you'll go to the dance?"

"I don't know." Jimmy Lee began slowly. "I'm not sure I'm ready to be in the same room with Mitch and Brenda for a whole evening. It's gotten easier seeing them together at school, but I still don't like it. Besides, I haven't been asked, and I doubt I will be."

"Don't be so sure," Reanna said. "Rick might ask you, or some other boy you haven't even thought about."

"Maybe," Jimmy Lee said quietly. Then she asked, "Have you looked up any of those scriptures we promised Kody?"

Reanna had, and the topic turned to a lively discussion of tithing.

That evening, when Jimmy Lee crawled into bed, Clover was already there.

CHAPTER 21

After sacrament meeting, Reanna, Jimmy Lee, and Kody met in the foyer.

"Here, read this!" exclaimed Reanna, handing Kody her Bible open to Malachi 3:10.

Kody read: " 'Bring ye all the tithes into the storehouse, that there may be meat in mine house, and prove me now herewith, saith the Lord of hosts, if I will not open you the windows of heaven, and pour you out a blessing, that there shall not be room enough to receive it.' "

"There are others too," Jimmy Lee added. She unfolded a sheet of paper with her references on it.

"And here's one from the Book of Mormon," Reanna said. "Alma 13:15. 'And it was this same Melchizedek to whom Abraham paid tithes; yea even our father Abraham paid tithes of one-tenth part of all he possessed.' "

She looked at Kody and said seriously, "I guess it boils down to one thing. Do you believe that the scriptures are the word of God?"

Kody furrowed his brow and then looked at both girls. "I think so, but I'm not sure. I do believe there is a God."

Both girls were silent. This was a monumental statement for Kody, who just weeks ago was asking if there was a God. Finally Jimmy Lee smiled. "You're beginning to build on faith, Kody. How does it feel?"

"Warm," Kody replied. "It feels warm."

They began to walk toward their Sunday School class.

"How are your folks feeling about the missionary discussions now?" Reanna asked.

"Well, I think they're both trying to understand my pull towards it," said Kody slowly. "I think they see it as a phase. I know they're worried that it'll take me away from my family. My mom is really having a hard time. Dad tries harder to understand."

"It's nice of him to attend the missionary meetings and support you, Kody, even though he doesn't understand."

"Yes, it really is," sighed Kody. "But there's so much I don't understand myself."

Reanna put her hand on his arm. "It'll be okay, Kody," she said gently.

Kody smiled. His skin tingled where Reanna had placed her hand. As they settled down in class he stole a sideways glance at Reanna. She was wearing a spring pink dress with matching shoes and that same tantalizing perfume. She was the perfect picture of femininity, and he felt an irresistible attraction to her. He wanted to ask her to the spring dance. But he wasn't quite sure how to go about it. And what would Jimmy Lee think? He still could remember the surprise on her face when she caught him in his romantic fantasy about Reanna.

But Jimmy Lee and her family usually left first. If he hung around, there would be a moment when he would have Reanna all to himself. He'd ask her today.

After church, he and Reanna were waving good-bye to Jimmy Lee and her family as they pulled out of the parking lot. Kody turned to Reanna. He knew he'd only have a minute before her parents called. Suddenly his palms began to sweat and he could feel his mouth twitching. He pressed his lips shut, swallowed, and impulsively took Reanna's hand, ignoring her shocked look.

"Reenie," he began, "I'd be honored if you'd attend the spring dance with me in two weeks."

Reanna looked at him with wide eyes, biting her lip. Gently

she squeezed Kody's hand and managed a smile. "Kody, you've completely surprised me," she said softly, "and I'm truly flattered you would even consider me, but I can't go with you. Eric Miller asked me just last Friday and I told him yes."

Kody's mind whirled. Who was Eric Miller? "I'm sorry," he stammered. "I guess . . . I guess I don't know Eric."

Reanna gave a forced laugh. "He's from Eagleridge High. He goes to the Plum Hill Ward. I think you met him the day we worked on the church grounds."

Kody's mind was a blur. "Oh, of course," he said, not really remembering.

Reanna nodded. Then her eyes caught sight of her mother, beckoning her to the family car. Reanna gave Kody a desperate look as she let go of his hand. "I'll see you tomorrow, won't I?"

Kody tried to give her a cheerful smile. "You bet," he replied.

Reanna turned and walked across the parking lot. Kody watched her leave and saw her turn and wave one last time. He forced himself to wave back cheerfully. What was he going to do? He'd made a complete idiot of himself. Closing his eyes, he heaved a sigh and dragged himself to his car.

How would this change things? Would Reanna even speak to him after this? What about Jimmy Lee? She'd probably be furious with him for ruining a perfect threesome. And how did he feel? Mostly stupid for even thinking Reanna would consider going to the dance with him. He had been willing to trade her warmth and friendship for the possibility of something more, but now it was obvious that her interests lay elsewhere.

As Kody walked into the house he tried to put on a happier face but his mother spotted his anxiety.

"What's the matter?" she asked. "Did something happen at church?"

"I asked Reanna to the spring dance and she said no," he blurted out. "She's already going with someone. Someone who's—" Kody stopped himself before announcing that Eric was a Mormon.

"Oh, Kody, honey, I'm sorry," his mother said. "I've wondered about your true feelings for Reanna."

"Well, I've tried to keep them to myself, but today I decided I was just going to risk it and—well, I guess I blew it."

"Now, don't talk like that. The two of you are great friends, and I'm sure she'll want to continue to be your friend. The question is, how do you feel about her? Do you still want to be her friend?"

"Yeah, I do."

"What does Jimmy Lee say?"

"She doesn't know yet, but I'm sure Reanna will call her sometime today and tell her about it."

"Now, Son, don't worry about this. Reanna and Jimmy Lee are sensitive young women. I'm sure it'll all be fine. Is there someone else you'd like to ask to the spring dance?"

Kody shook his head. "No. I don't think I'll go."

"Well, give it a couple of days," Vonnie suggested. "You might change your mind."

Kody flopped onto the couch and his mother sat beside him. "I'd like to ask you another question," Vonnie said. "Kody, all along I've wondered if maybe your feelings for these young women haven't been the motivation behind your interest in their religion. That's pretty clear, isn't it? I've wondered if maybe you thought you'd have a better chance at getting Reanna's attention if you were LDS."

Kody shook his head. He didn't feel like talking about it now, but he didn't want his mother to entertain the wrong idea. "I can see why you'd think those things, Mom, but it's not the case."

"You mentioned that Reanna was going to the dance with someone else? Is this boy LDS?"

Kody nodded. "Yes. But that doesn't have anything to do with me."

"Sometimes, Kody, when we're involved in a situation, it's hard to see it clearly. I'd suggest you back away from this religious study for a while and see how you feel. You may get a whole new perspective."

Panic started to grow inside of Kody. "No," he stated. "I can't do that. I've learned so much, and I'm so close."

"So close to what?" Vonnie asked.

Kody shook his head. "I'm not sure. Close to that discovery I've told you about." He paused. "I know one thing for certain. There is a God."

Vonnie looked perplexed. "How do you *know* for certain?"

"I've done what the elders have asked. I'm reading the Book of Mormon and I've been praying and now I know there's a God."

Vonnie furrowed her brow. "Kody," she began, "sometimes when we want something, we can make it seem so, even if it's not true."

"That's not the case, Mom. I understand what you're saying, but I've worked hard on this and I'm learning new things all the time. It's wonderful. I wish you'd attend the lessons with me."

"Your father gives me a rundown of everything you've been taught. To be honest, I can't buy the first vision stuff. To me that makes the whole outfit a sham." She held up her hand to keep Kody from protesting. "I know you feel differently and I think the Donovans are very nice people. Gullible but nice. So, I don't see any point in my attending."

"But, Mom, the elders could answer your questions, if you'd just give them a chance."

"I don't have any questions, Kody."

Kody looked down at his lap. "I'm playing in sacrament meeting next month. I think they want me to play for Easter Sunday. Will you come and listen to me play?"

Kody could tell his mother was surprised. "But you're not a member of their church. Why would they ask you to play?"

"Reenie told Brother Simpson about me and he said they're always looking for musical numbers to add to the spirit of their meeting. I've been around so much and everyone is so accepting that I don't think it matters if I'm a member or not."

Vonnie was thoughtful for a moment. "Okay, Kody. I'll come hear you play. Have you told your father this?"

"Not yet. But I'll ask him, too."

Vonnie patted her son's knee. "You need to practice this afternoon. I'm going to start dinner, so why don't you heat up a bowl of soup and then you can practice for a while."

"Okay, Mom." Kody rose from the couch. As he was about to leave the room he turned back to face his mother. "Oh, and Mom? Thanks."

Vonnie searched her son's face for a moment before nodding. "You're welcome, Kody," she said.

A few minutes later, Kody was warming up on his arpeggios. The new feeling of warmth and acceptance filled him. In all the years Kody had been playing the oboe, never before had he gleaned so much satisfaction from his music. It was as if the old dream of being a sports hero didn't matter quite so much anymore. Was it because of what Mr. Svenson was trying to teach him? One thing was certain—this was where his strength lay and it was important.

Suddenly, Kody stopped playing. Could it be that his Heavenly Father was pleased with the music Kody made? Placing his instrument on the bed, Kody knelt down and began the pattern of prayer that was still new to him. The answer came in a resounding *yes*. His Heavenly Father was pleased with Kody's effort to make beautiful music. Kody was so sure he heard a voice that he opened his eyes, so he could catch a glimpse of who was speaking. But he was only greeted by the afternoon sun slanting through his window and a gentle breeze rustling the tree near his room. Still, the feeling remained. Someone had spoken to him!

Rising from his kneeling position, Kody once again picked up his oboe. He began to play with such profound joy that tears streamed down his face, making it difficult to see the music. His oboe was a means of communication. His music had the ear of God! Kody was overwhelmed. Once again he put down his oboe. He simply couldn't play anymore. The tears were coming too fast and sobs were wrenching his throat. He could scarcely believe it. He hadn't cried since he was a baby, but he could not resist the bursting joy that was so strong that tears were the only way he could express it.

After the emotional storm was over, Kody blew his nose, went in the bathroom and washed his face, then put his oboe away, almost reverently. He propped his pillow against the headboard of his bed and made himself comfortable. A new and peaceful calm enveloped him. His mind was clear and unhindered. Pulling the Book of Mormon and the Bible from the shelf, he took out the paper Jimmy Lee had given him with references to tithing. Slowly he began to look up each one. As he read, he searched his mind for negative feelings. None came. Instead, he had the desire to give whatever he could to the Lord. Surely, his music was an acceptable gift. So was 10 percent of whatever he earned. It wasn't really that much. Kody's father's words sounded dim in Kody's ears now. There were reasons for tithing. The scriptures pointed out several of them. Kody felt a deep satisfaction.

Carefully, Kody also read the other material the elders had given him throughout his lessons. He re-read the Joseph Smith story and the pages on the plan of salvation. All of it fell into place. Kody realized that indeed he had discovered treasure. He had discovered the truth.

Then, just before he was about to put his study materials away, Kody found a scripture marked on the back of Jimmy Lee's page.

> *Doctrine and Covenants 84:82–83. "Consider the lilies of the field, how they grow, . . . and the kingdoms of the world, in all their glory, are not arrayed like one of these. For your Father, who is in heaven, knoweth that you have need of all these things."*

Kody closed his eyes. It made perfect sense. His Father in Heaven knew that he needed his oboe and the gospel.

CHAPTER 22

Kody spotted the girls at their usual cafeteria table and made his way through the milling crowd. He felt lucky to find a seat across from them. They seemed tense. Had asking Reanna to the spring dance permanently damaged their bond of friendship? But in any case he had to tell them something much more important. "I need to talk to the two of you privately," he said, raising his voice to be heard over the din of the cafeteria.

Jimmy Lee and Reanna looked at each other with worried glances but both followed him outside. The fitful March breeze had kept most of the students inside, and the three friends sat down at a picnic table. He could feel the news bubbling up in his chest. He knew he was grinning. "I want to be baptized."

Reanna broke into a relieved grin, and Jimmy Lee exulted. "Kody, that's wonderful! When did you come to this conclusion?"

"Yesterday afternoon," Kody said. "After I got home from church I started to play my oboe and, well, I—" Kody could feel the tears welling up behind his eyes once again, and he couldn't speak.

"It's okay, Kody," Reanna said. "We understand. Don't we Jimmy Lee?"

Jimmy Lee nodded.

Kody smiled. "What's the next step?"

Reanna answered. "When we meet with the missionaries on Wednesday you need to tell them and they'll set it up."

"Have you told your folks?" Jimmy Lee asked.

Kody nodded solemnly. "I told them last night."

"What did they say?"

"I think they're trying to understand, but I know they're not happy. To be honest, they haven't given their permission. Will I need it?"

Both girls nodded.

Kody looked crestfallen.

Jimmy Lee squeezed Kody's hand. "Kody, you wouldn't want to be baptized without their consent. It would come between you, and the Church doesn't stand for that."

"What exactly did they say?" Reanna asked.

"Well, they didn't exactly say no. Mom cried and said she was afraid I'd want to serve a mission and that I'd never come home. She thinks my membership will take me away from the family—that eventually we'll just drift apart and the Church will become my family." Kody didn't tell the girls that his mother was convinced that his feelings for Reanna were behind his decision.

"My dad wonders why I have to look outside my family to have my needs fulfilled." Kody sighed. "I've tried to explain to them that the gospel won't change my relationship with them and that they're great parents, but I think they see this as some huge failure on their part. Also, they say that the gospel has already changed my relationship with them. I used to spend Sunday at home and now I spend it at church. They're really touchy about that."

Reanna and Jimmy Lee looked sad. "This must be incredibly hard for your folks, Kody," Jimmy Lee said.

"One good thing happened yesterday," Kody said with animation. "Both my mom and my dad said they'd come to church to hear me play on Easter Sunday."

"That's great," Reanna said. "Maybe then they'll relax and give their consent."

"Oh, Reanna, you're such an optimist," groaned Jimmy Lee.

"I think she's a pessimist," said Kody. "I don't want to wait a month to be baptized."

Both girls nodded their understanding.

An hour later, amid the beakers and black tables of the science room, Kody and Jimmy Lee worked on their latest experiment. After several minutes Jimmy Lee put down her glass of hydrogen peroxide and looked Kody straight in the eye. "There's something I have to ask you," she said as she sat down.

Kody sat down in his chair.

"Reanna told me what happened yesterday after church. I'm sorry she turned you down, Kody. I wish I'd warned you sooner. Reanna is an incredible flirt. She's my best friend and I love her dearly, but she's always been this way. Even in grade school, when most girls hate boys, Reanna couldn't leave them alone."

Kody grinned. "That doesn't surprise me."

"I guess I'm concerned that you've made this sudden decision to be baptized after she told you about Eric. I'm afraid you might think you'll feel like you have more in common with Reanna and can get her attention if you're baptized." She paused and looked at the floor. "Or something like that."

"You're not the only one who worries about my feelings for Reanna, Jimmy Lee," said Kody. "My mother is convinced that Reanna is the reason for my decision to be baptized."

"Oh, Kody, I'm sorry. I didn't mean to—"

"No, Jimmy Lee. I understand. But Reanna *isn't* my reason for wanting to be baptized. I had an amazing experience yesterday. I can't describe it, really, but I've studied and I've prayed and I know it's true."

Jimmy Lee visibly relaxed. "I'm happy for you, Kody. I really am."

He grinned back. "See why I have to be baptized?"

"What about your folks?"

"I don't know. They can withhold their permission for

now, but I turn eighteen in July. That's only four months away. Either way, I'll be baptized."

Later that evening Rick called. Jimmy Lee was delighted to talk about Clover's antics and growth. Rick was an enthusiastic participant. He listened and laughed with Jimmy Lee and told his own stories about Polar when she was a puppy. The conversation was fun, even if Clover was trying to eat the receiver.

"I was wondering if you'd want to go to the spring dance with me?" Rick asked.

Jimmy Lee held her breath before speaking. "Rick, I really appreciate your asking me. You don't know how much I appreciate it—but I don't think I'll be going."

"Why not?" he asked, then added hastily, "It's none of my business. I'm sorry."

"Oh, no," she blurted out. "I just don't want to be in the same room with Mitch and Brenda. To be stuck at a dance with the two of them is just more than I think I can handle."

Rick was quiet for a moment. "I guess I can understand how you feel." He hesitated. "Jimmy Lee, would you mind if I asked someone else? I really would like to go."

"Oh, Rick, not at all," she said, relieved. "Truly, I wouldn't mind at all. I had a wonderful time with you, and I hope we can spend more time together, but that shouldn't keep you from taking someone else to the dance."

"I'm glad you feel that way. I want you to know, Jimmy Lee, that you're my first choice for a date to the dance. If you want a couple of days to think about it. . . ."

"No, Rick, really. I do appreciate the invitation. I truly do, but I think I'll just stay home and spend the evening with my family. Have a great time. And come over anytime and see Clover."

Jimmy Lee smiled as she hung up. This was good, she decided; to have friends like Rick, and Kody—friends she would never know if she were still dating Mitch. The thought made her feel warm and surprisingly grown-up.

Later that evening, over hot chocolate, Jimmy Lee told her parents about Kody's decision to be baptized and the upset to his parents.

"It'll all work out," Beth said as she patted Jimmy Lee's hand. "If Kody is truly committed, then he'll eventually be baptized. The Lord will see to it."

Jimmy Lee nodded silently.

"We can all discuss it with the elders tomorrow night. Possibly his father will feel differently," Beth said hopefully.

"I hope so, Mom," Jimmy Lee said.

Beth changed the subject. "What about the spring dance the weekend after next? Are you excited?"

Jimmy Lee laughed. "Oh, Mom, you act as if I'm going for sure."

"Well, you are, aren't you?"

"No," Jimmy Lee said firmly. "Rick asked me tonight on the phone but I turned him down."

"Why?" Wes asked. "He seemed very nice and you said you enjoyed his company."

"Oh, I did," Jimmy Lee exclaimed. "I was very flattered he asked me, but I'm just not ready to spend an evening watching Mitch and Brenda, and that's exactly how it would feel. I'm sure I wouldn't be able to focus on anyone else."

"You haven't seen Mitch in almost three months. Why would that bother you?" Wes asked.

"I see him at school sometimes," Jimmy Lee explained. "And it still bothers me."

"Well, I'm sorry you won't be going," Beth said. "I saw the prettiest dress downtown this afternoon and it's just perfect for you."

"Thanks, Mom. Maybe next time," Jimmy Lee said.

In her room, Jimmy Lee picked up the pictures she still clung to. She could remember the sound of Mitch's voice and the way his light brown eyes were flecked with black. When would the vividness of such recollections leave her?

In Mitch's room their prom picture stood on the small entertainment stand. It had been tacked to the wall until she bought a frame. Had he replaced their picture with a photo of him and Brenda? Would Brenda have to buy a frame or would he just throw away the photo of him with Jimmy Lee and reuse the frame?

She placed her photo face down on her nightstand and considered placing it in the manila envelope that was in her closet. No, she wasn't ready for that. Not yet. Quietly, she hugged Clover.

CHAPTER 23

Kody sat in Mr. Svenson's studio and played his warm-up scales.

Mr. Svenson raised his eyebrows. "Kody, have you lengthened your practice sessions?" he asked.

"Some."

"I can tell that you've been working on playing phrases instead of just notes. Even your scales were round and full of life."

Kody grinned. "I think I'm ready to play a treasure today, Mr. Svenson."

Mr. Svenson placed the music on the stand. "I'm listening."

Kody studied the music for a moment. Then he began the piece by Haydn. Its exuberance and thrill mimicked what was pulsing in Kody's heart. With the excitement of an explorer he phrased his notes to sound light and full of hope. After his last note faded, he turned to Mr. Svenson.

His music teacher was beaming. "Kody, that is the best I've ever heard you play. It was tremendous. You interpreted the music and made it come to life. You're beginning to discover your own unique style."

Kody smiled. "I've decided to be baptized, Mr. Svenson, and I've never been so happy in all my life."

"Well, that happiness is showing through your music, Kody, and it's just wonderful."

"I'm going to play in church on Easter Sunday."

"Perfect. I couldn't think of a better place for you to explore your treasure than in a church."

For several minutes Kody and Mr. Svenson worked over the finer pieces of the music. Then as Kody was putting his oboe away he turned to his music teacher. "You know, Mr. Svenson, the oboe really is a beautiful instrument, isn't it."

Mr. Svenson smiled. "Yes, Kody. It's the most beautiful instrument there is."

The following day, before school, Kody opened his locker and unrolled his new poster. He had gone to the music store after his lesson and picked up a picture of an oboe against bright, jazzy colors. Vivid blues, deep purples, and stunning magenta swept the background while the oboe stood in front, its polished wooden body the perfect background for shiny silver keys. Notes swirled on the paper, as if following some unseen breeze. Kody thought it would fit perfectly. But when he unrolled it he realized that it was bigger than he had thought. If he unrolled it to its full length it would cover most of his poster of Jerry Rice.

Kody stepped back from his open locker door. What should he do? It didn't take him long to decide. It was time for the action shot of Jerry Rice to come down. He had lugged it through two years of high school. It was time for a change.

Pulling gently at the corner, Kody propped the poster of the Jerry Rice picture against his leg as he hung his new poster. It looked good.

"Hey, what are you going to do with that Jerry Rice poster?" a passing student asked.

Kody shrugged. "I don't know. Do you want it?"

"Yeah!"

Kody handed the poster to the sophomore.

"Thanks!" he said. "I've been wanting one of these for a while."

"I hope you enjoy it."

Carefully the student rolled it up and walked down the hall.

The buzzer rang and Kody hurriedly picked the books he would need for first period. He took one last look at the oboe poster before he closed the door. It belonged.

CHAPTER 24

The Sunday after the dance, Jimmy Lee climbed out of the car at church and hurried to the bulbs. No weeds here! Today she noticed the crocuses were in full bloom. Her heart quickened. For weeks she had been waiting for this wonderful event, and now it was beginning. The crocuses would be the first; the daffodils and hyacinths would come next; then her precious lilies. But would they bloom in time for Easter? It looked doubtful. Easter was only two weeks away and the buds were still tiny. She studied the little buds on the rest of the new plants and tried not to worry about the lilies.

"Jimmy Lee," Beth called from the door. "You'd better hurry."

Taking one last breath of the fresh, warm air, Jimmy Lee ducked inside the church.

When she was seated she looked around for Reanna and Kody. They were sitting with Reanna's family two rows up and to one side. Kody's father was with them. Jimmy Lee blinked. Michael McLaughlin was attending sacrament meeting! Jimmy Lee settled into her seat with a satisfied sigh. Her mother was right. The Lord was looking after Kody and his family. Kody's father was trying to understand. Hopefully it would help his parents accept Kody's desire to be baptized.

Reanna was looking at her and mouthing words. Jimmy Lee squinted at her best friend. Reanna was saying, "Got to talk. Urgent!"

Jimmy Lee nodded and relaxed.

After sacrament meeting Michael was going home, but he

wanted to speak to Kody. Apprehensively, Kody walked with him out to the car.

The spring sun was soft, and the breeze was scented with warmth and renewed life.

"Are you sure Jimmy Lee and her family won't mind bringing you home?" Michael asked. "I can come pick you up."

Kody shook his head. "They said it would be fine. It's not that far."

Michael nodded. "Kody, your mother and I have talked at length about this, and I think you know we're not real comfortable with your decision to join this church."

Kody didn't argue.

"I came to this meeting today so I could see for myself what Mormons do on Sunday, and I have to admit, I'm surprised."

"Why?"

Michael thought for a moment. "They're all so human."

"What did you expect?" Kody asked.

Michael shrugged. "I don't know. Priests in black robes. Monks in brown ones. I'm not sure. The meeting was much more casual than I expected. And everyone is so warm and kind. Is it the same everywhere you go?"

"I know the gospel doesn't change, but I'm not sure about the people. I've never been to another ward before."

"What do you mean when you say the gospel doesn't change?"

"What the elders have been teaching us, Dad, is the same lessons they teach in New York, Florida, and Kansas. The gospel is what I've been drawn to and it's the same no matter where you go."

Michael nodded then closed his eyes. "I won't pretend this is easy for us, Kody, because it's not. Your mother and I have always tried to be fair with you children, and this is no exception. Soon you'll be eighteen and you'll be making these kinds of decisions on your own, but I know how long four months can be when you're waiting for something important. It was like that for me when I married your mother." He sighed. "This is important to you, isn't it, Kody?"

Tears welled up in Kody's eyes. "Yes, Dad. It's the most important thing I've ever felt."

Michael looked at his son and then pulled him into an embrace. Kody hugged his father fiercely for a moment, then Michael placed his hands on his shoulders. "We won't stand in your way. If you want to join the Mormons, we'll support you. We don't understand, and I doubt we ever will, but we love you, Kody, and we want you to be happy."

Kody could feel the tears brimming over. He couldn't speak.

Michael opened the car door, then turned and looked at his son. "Do you remember when you asked me about faith? You asked me if I had faith in anything. Do you remember?"

Kody nodded.

"Well, Kody, I have faith in you." Michael looked intently at his son and then climbed into the car. Kody watched him drive away.

When Kody joined the two girls halfway through Sunday School, he was beaming. Without Kody saying a word, both girls knew why he was smiling. Jimmy Lee looked stunned and radiant simultaneously. Kody understood why when Reanna slipped him a note: "Mitch and Brenda broke up during the dance. GIANT fight in front of everybody!"

On Sunday afternoon Jimmy Lee was in her bedroom with Clover stretched out beside her. Her Bible was open, but she stared at the words without seeing them. Kody was going to be baptized! The news was almost more than Jimmy Lee could believe. Her thoughts bounced from Kody to Mitch. What did this breakup mean to her? Anything?

Her mother knocked and came in. Clover woke up and whuffled as Beth sat down on the bed. "So, how do you feel?"

"Well, Mom," Jimmy Lee began. "I'm not quite sure. It's like I'm on overload. One minute I'm excited for Kody, then I think of Mitch and Brenda breaking up and I get all confused.

I feel embarrassed for both Mitch and Brenda. I mean, that's such a tacky way to break up—and part of me feels malicious and wishes I had been there to see it, so I feel embarrassed that I'm so petty, and then—well, the strange thing is, I don't feel much of anything at all. I mean, for weeks now I've been praying and wishing this would happen, and now that it has it doesn't matter. Then I think of Kody again and I get excited. Does this make any sense?"

Beth laughed. "Sure it does. But sort it out after dinner, okay? We're almost ready to eat."

Jimmy Lee grinned.

CHAPTER 25

Standing in the parking lot of the school grounds, Jimmy Lee impatiently rummaged through the mess in the back seat of Reanna's car. She had left her chemistry notebook in the car and now she was frantic. Class would be starting any minute. What if she couldn't find it?

Her eye caught the corner of her blue notebook and relief flooded through her. She pulled it out from a pile of papers and Reanna's cosmetic kit.

"Jimmy Lee," a boy's voice said. It was Mitch.

Jimmy Lee jumped, cracking her head on the door frame. "Ow," she said, rubbing her head. She felt embarrassed and was trying hard not to look shocked.

"I'm sorry," Mitch said sympathetically. "I didn't mean to startle you. I should've waited until you were finished, I guess."

"I'll be fine," Jimmy Lee responded. "What can I do for you, Mitch?" She was surprised at how calm her voice sounded.

Mitch hesitated, looking over the parking lot. Then he looked directly at Jimmy Lee. The black flecks in his bright brown eyes caught the sunlight. "I was wondering if you'd want to go to the movies or something this Friday night?"

Jimmy Lee was stunned. "What are you saying?"

Mitch took a deep breath. "I'm asking you out for a date, I guess."

Jimmy Lee looked down at her feet, her thoughts in chaos. How did she feel about dating Mitch? Asking the question gave her the answer. Their relationship had gone way beyond a casual evening out. "I don't think so," she replied softly.

Mitch smiled uneasily. "You're not going to make this easy on me, are you?" he asked as he shifted on his feet.

"I'm not trying to be difficult," she began.

Mitch took a deep breath. "Jimmy Lee," he said earnestly. "I'd like for us to get back together. You know, how it used to be. We used to have a wonderful time. Remember how we used to go cross-country skiing with Ruff? And all those basketball games you used to cheer me through? Those victories were as much yours as mine." He shrugged. "I miss all of that. I miss you."

Jimmy Lee looked away. She'd dreamed of this moment, but now she didn't want it. Why not? Slowly she realized that she didn't really want things to be as they were before: the arguments and tension over sex, the exclusion of Reanna and her other friends, Mitch's refusal to share her life at church . . . When had she stopped missing him? Shaking her head slowly, she answered, "No, Mitch. Things would never be the same between us."

"Look, I know I've made some drastic mistakes and I'm really sorry, Jimmy Lee. You don't know how sorry. Do you think you could ever find it in your heart to forgive me?"

Jimmy Lee sighed. "Forgiveness really isn't the issue. I think I've forgiven you, but I could never trust you again."

"Maybe we could start slow and take it just one evening at a time. Would that suit you?"

"Listen, Mitch, I appreciate what you're saying, and maybe you've learned something from it all, but you're not the only one that's learned and changed, Mitch. I have, too, and I just don't think we'd be very compatible anymore."

"It's Kody McLaughlin isn't it? Or maybe it's Rick Morris," Mitch said bitterly.

"No, Mitch. It's you and it's me. I'm not the same Jimmy Lee you used to date and I doubt you'd like me very much." The late bell rang and Jimmy Lee shifted her books. She didn't want to be too late for class.

"I've got to go," she said locking the car door.

"We'll talk again," Mitch said.

Jimmy Lee turned to face Mitch. "We don't have anything to say to one another, Mitch." Then she walked away.

Later that afternoon Jimmy Lee sat at her writing desk and tried to concentrate on her homework, but her eyes were drawn to the picture on her nightstand. Carefully she unlatched the back of the frame and removed the picture and placed it in the manila envelope.

Once again she dipped into the pictures and looked over slices of her life. Then she looked around the room one more time. Nothing remained of Mitch, except what she had in the envelope. She carefully sealed it shut and then walked out to the garage with Clover at her heels, where she placed the envelope in the garbage.

One of these days she would have her folks take some pictures of her, Reanna, Kody, and Clover to decorate her room, but until then she would just have to look at blank walls.

CHAPTER 26

Kody cradled the Easter lily in his arm as he walked toward the church. It was Easter Sunday and he couldn't wait to give Jimmy Lee her present.

He studied the bell-like flowers. They did kind of look like his oboe.

"Are you ready to play your solo?" Vonnie asked.

"I think so," Kody said. He was surprised that he didn't feel a bit nervous. "Thanks for coming, Mom and Dad. I really appreciate you being here."

"We told you we'd come hear you play," Vonnie said. "And a McLaughlin never goes back on their word. Besides, I've attended every solo you've ever performed. I'm not going to stop now."

Kody smiled. Well, that was one way to get his family to church. He wondered if he would be playing often.

He spotted the Donovans' car. "There's Jimmy Lee. I need to give this to her before church."

"Hurry up," Michael said. "You don't want to be late for your performance."

Kody handed his oboe case and music to his mother, then hurried toward Jimmy Lee. They stopped short of the entrance.

"You ready for your big moment?" Wes asked.

"Absolutely," Kody replied. "Jimmy Lee, may I speak with you for a moment?"

She glanced at her folks.

"Don't be long," Wes said.

Both Kody and Jimmy Lee watched her family walk into the church, where they met the McLaughlins.

"Come look at the flowers," Jimmy Lee said as she headed across the lawn.

Kody followed. "They're beautiful."

"Remember that day when it was cold and gray and we were out here spreading this bark dust?"

"I'll never forget it. It was my first introduction to the church."

Jimmy Lee smiled. "I think we've come a long way since then, Kody. What do you think?"

Kody nodded.

"I'm glad to see your folks here. How are they feeling about your baptism next week?"

Kody shrugged. "Dad said he'd come. Mom hasn't said yet. I'm hoping she'll decide to come after today." He handed Jimmy Lee the Easter lily. "I know you like these. I thought I'd give you one for Easter," he said shyly.

Tears flooded Jimmy Lee's eyes. "Oh, Kody. It's beautiful. The Easter lilies we've planted haven't bloomed yet, and I was feeling a bit sad about that. They mean so much to me."

"I know. There's a card inside."

Jimmy Lee found the white envelope with gold trim. Inside was a tiny card.

> *Doctrine and Covenants 84:82–83. "Consider the lilies of the field, how they grow, . . . and the kingdoms of the world, in all their glory, are not arrayed like one of these. For your Father, who is in heaven, knoweth that you have need of all these things."*

"I found this scripture on the back of the paper you gave me with your tithing references," Kody said quietly. "And I remember that night I played for you and Reanna; you asked me to play lilies in a field, but I couldn't do it."

"I remember."

"Well, today, Jimmy Lee, I'll be playing lilies in a field, or at least my version of them."

Jimmy Lee put her arm around her friend and gave him a hug. "I can't wait," she said.

As they reached the door of the church, Jimmy Lee took one more look at the mild spring day. It was hard to believe that winter had ever had its gray grip on the beautiful landscape. Winter had also lived in her heart. But not anymore! Like her surroundings, Jimmy Lee had reached for the sun and the warmth of the gospel, and it had been there.

ABOUT THE AUTHOR

Shelly Johnson-Choong was born in Las Vegas, Nevada, and educated in the Pacific Northwest. She has lectured in her community and often participates as a speaker in LDS youth firesides. In addition to many Church callings in the Young Women organization, she has enjoyed serving as a stake missionary, Compassionate Service teacher in the Relief Society, as well as a temple ordinance worker. She is currently serving as a Gospel Doctrine teacher.

She is also the author of *The Jewelry Box* and *A Light to Come Home By.*

She enjoys traveling abroad with her husband, Larry, and exploring the Pacific Northwest with her beloved dog, Koshi. Shelly also enjoys her music; as a flutist, she has studied with some of the finest musicians in the Northwest and she performs often.

She is a former equestrian and entrepreneur, and loves observing wildlife. She takes care of wild birds and enjoys watching them raise their families. Her greatest joys, however, are her family and friends.